Scriabin for Neuroscientists

Lazaros C. Triarhou

Scriabin for Neuroscientists

A Study in Syn-Aesthetics

CORPUS CALLOSUM
Thessalonica · Indianapolis

Scriabin for neuroscientists : a study in syn-aesthetics.

A Corpus Callosum book published by

Lazaros C. Triarhou, MD PhD
Professor of Neuroscience
University of Macedonia
Egnatia 156
Thessalonica 54006 (Greece)

LIBRARY OF CONGRESS CONTROL NUMBER: 2015943337

Cataloging-in-Publication Data

Triarhou, Lazaros Constantinos
    Scriabin for neuroscientists : a study in syn-aesthetics / Lazaros C. Triarhou.
    p. cm.
    Includes bibliographical references.
    LCCN 2015943337
    ISBN-13: 978-1-5142-0206-7
    ISBN-10: 1-5142-0206-9

    1. Scriabin, Alexander, 1872–1915. 2. Composers—Russia—Biography. 3. Pianists—Russia—Biography.   I. Title.

Printed in the United States of America

The Corpus Callosum logo is based on a drawing by the neurobiologist Christofredo Jakob from his *Icones Neurologicae* (1897).

The work of humans ought to be the creation and living
of the entire Nature and then of the entire Cosmos;
the Universe must be the expression and the realisation
of a unified musical state of being and, if you agree,
be the music of existence itself.

—Alexander N. Scriabin

CONTENTS

INTRODUCTION

THE PIANIST AND COMPOSER Alexander N. Scriabin
(1872–1915) is an isolated phenomenon in Russian
music [Altschuler, 1972], an almost inconceivable ex-
ception unique in the history of music, who erected
classical edifices of sound, fashioned in a perfectly finished form, consistent within themselves, but independent in the classical sense [de Schloezer, 1987]. Today he is part of the mainstream of music in Russian
conservatories [Bowers, 1972].

In his last works, he searched for a new musical language, abandoned tonality, experimentally used colours, and delved into innumerable innovations in various branches of art, scenery, lighting, plastic movement, all paths that logically anticipate the experimen-
tation of contemporary artists; many of those ideas
have become standard features on our horizon, yet they
were already discernible in 1910 in the fascinating mu-

sical cosmos of Scriabin [Scriabine, 1987].

The most extraordinary aspect of Scriabin's cognitive striving was his perseverance toward maximum clarity; everything in his discourse was lucid, transparent, and precise in concept [de Schloezer, 1987]. As a piano virtuoso he was admired; that extraordinary talent gives a clue to the enormous pianistic qualities of his comositions [Bowers, 1972]. He had a variety of touches, and his manipulation of the pedal was a revelation [Altschuler, 1972]. He never resorted to improvisation; he would either plunge into new compositions or play his old pieces. As a composer, he paced the floor entire long nights thinking out his compositions; any sound, all sounds, were consciously realised and recorded in his memory [Altschuler, 1972] intuitively perceived as focal lights [de Schloezer, 1987]. In states of new visions he seemed intoxicated by the potency of creative ecstasy, possessed by a mysterious force, dissolved in his spirit, transfigured.

His life even inspired a novel by screenwriter Friedrich N. Gorenstein (1932–2002). The story [Gorenstein, 1992] opens and concludes with an extract from Scriabin's notes: "Monuments and dreams are made of the same stuff, and both appear equally real. An unrealised dream is an unidentified object at a distance." In between, the novelist reconstructs the life of a composer who incarnated the will to transform the world through the power of a total art, his "new gospel," a synthesis of music, philosophy and religion. Some were able to salute his singularity, experiencing in chills "the kisses he gave to sounds," the vibrations of new harmonies he brought forth. Scriabin, a nervous nature, irritable, fragile, with much work unfinished, exemplifies the voluntary principle of all true creation.

Scriabin is reckoned one of music's revolutionaries; his music has been qualified as genial, completely personal, scintillantly novel, eloquent, articulate, impassioned, transcendental and ecstatic, an art capable of transforming life to endless beneficence [Mann, 1980]. Perfection marks every Scriabin piece [de Schloezer, 1987]. In addition to composing music, he wrote poems, such as the text for *Le poème de l'extase* and *Acte préalable*.

Papers that discuss the phenomenon of synaesthesia often mention the case of Scriabin. Synaesthesia is the involuntary physical experience of a cross-modal linkage; for example, the hearing of a tone ('inducing stimulus') elicits the sensation of seeing a colour (the 'concurrent perception'), in the absence of a direct stimulation of the visual receptors [Beeli et al., 2005]. Such an experience is a genuine perception, not a memory or a learned or metaphorical association, and is reproducible throughout one's life-span [Pearce, 2007]. Estimates of the prevalence of true synaesthesia in the general population range from 1 in 25,000 to 1 in 500, with a likely average of 1 in 2,000 individuals [Cytowic, 1989; Harrison, 2001].

In its strict neurological definition, synaesthesia entails the *automatic* and *consistent* coupling of different sensory modalities, as result of a presumed differentiation failure in brain development. A common coupling is the auditory-visual, where the subject experiences the sight of a specific colour (wave-length) at the sound of a specific note (sound frequency).

Synaesthesia has been described in artists, including composers, such as Nikolai Rimsky-Korsakov, Franz Liszt, Jean Sibelius, and Olivier Messiaen. On the other hand, for literary scholars and artists, the synaesthetic experience often implies an imagery of combined senses, in other words, a multisensory blend in a metaphor or an artistic work; as a matter of fact, some kinds of imagery are inherently multisensory in ways that go beyond the common definitions of synaesthesia [Starr, 2013]. In this book I revisit the issue of Scriabin's "coloured tonality."

Scriabin's interest in colour apparently began in 1907, when, at the age of 35 and in a conversation with Rimsky-Korsakov, found that they both associated colours, albeit different, with specific pitch. That was a period marked by the great surge of interest in the 'artistic' synaesthesia that the European avant-garde displayed between Baudelaire and Rimbaud, by the triumphant progress of cinematography and its domination of the visual media. Attempts to evoke the experience of one sense by an appeal to another were common and musical images in painting and poetry were common: Whistler painted nocturnes, Debussy composed images, while the remoter fringe of synaesthetic experi ments produced smell-keyboards and colour-organs against a background of limitless scientific optimism. The potential of such machines seemed at least as promising as that of the typewriter, the magic lantern, and other new-fangled fruits of mechanical ingenuity. Scriabin was convinced that the experience of colours would enhance the experience of sounds, and suggested that an audience would absorb *Prometheus* more fully if it were bathed in coloured light corresponding throughout to the harmonic flow of the music. In Scriabin's usage, the art of abstract colours over the dimension of time, which had not even been developed for the cinema yet, is exceedingly primitive, in contrast with the music, which is exceedingly sophisticated [Macdonald, 1978].

THE COMPOSER

ALEXANDER NIKOLAEVICH SCRIABIN (figure 1) was born at 2 p.m. (Moscow time) on 6 January 1872 — or Christmas Day 1871 according to the Julian calendar, effective in old Russia before 1900 — to Nikolai Alexandrovich Scriabin (1850-1914), a diplomat, and Lubov Alexandrovna Shchetinina (1849-1873), a reputed pianist and pupil of Polish composer Teodor Leszetycki (1830-1915) at the Saint Petersburg Conservatory [de Schloezer, 1987].

Scriabin was a child prodigy and revealed striking musical abilities. At age 11 he joined the Second Cadet Corps, a military academy in Lefortovo, and obtained a finishing diploma in 1889.

His first piano lessons were taken privately from composer and violinist Georges E. Conus (1862-1933), who was Professor of Theory, Harmony and Orchestration. He entered the Moscow Conservatory in 1888 where he continued the piano instruction under Nikolai S. Zverev (1832–1893) and Vassily I. Safonov (1852–1918), the greatest Muscovite teachers of the time. Both saw through the striking originality of Scriabin, and both regarded the young pupil as their favourite [Altschuler, 1972]. He also studied music theory and counterpoint with Sergei I. Taneyev (1856–1915), who had followed Tchaikovsky as the Principal of the Conservatory in 1882, and composition and fugue with Anton S. Arensky (1861–1906) [Eaglefield Hull, 1916b].

Scriabin graduated in 1892 in piano with the Gold Medal. The 'Gold Tablets' at the Conservatory also register the other three graduates who won the Gold Medal that year (the 23rd annual graduation): J. Lhévinne, L. Maximov and S. Rachmaninoff [Belsa, 1986].

Arensky did not sign Scriabin's piano diploma, neither did Scriabin receive a diploma in composition, because the young student had not complied with his teacher's request to compose an opera, coming up instead with a *Scherzo*, and subsequently a five-voiced *Fugue* which today is part of the required curriculum throughout Russian conservatories [Bowers, 1972].

Figure 1 Left, Scriabin in 1903 [Rudakova and Kandinsky, 1980]. The photo is rare, considering that the composer "never wore a hat" [Altschuler, 1972]. Signature etched digitally onto the photo from a letter to publisher Belaïeff, dated 11 February 1895 [Franke, 1973]. Upper right, Nikolai Zverev among his pupils: Scriabin, K. M. Chernyaev, Matvey Presman (sitting, left to right), and Semyon Samuelson, Leonid Maximov, Sergei Rachmaninoff and Fyodor Koeneman (standing, left to right). Lower right, Scriabin's graduation diploma in piano from the Moscow Conservatory [Rudakova and Kandinsky, 1980].

Five years later, Scriabin was appointed as the youngest Professor of Piano at the Moscow Conservatory. During that time he composed the *Piano Concerto in F-sharp minor*, op. 20. He resigned his position in 1903, as he became bored, declaring, "I cannot bear to hear other people's music all day, and I write my own at night" [Hope, 1970].

Two injuries caused young Alexander to practise on the piano with his left hand alone [Gunst, 1916] and to remain anxious throughout his life regarding the stamina of his right hand [Altenmüller, 2015]. Those periods of convalescence may account in some measure for the difficulty of the left-hand parts in many of his pieces [Eaglefield Hull, 1916b]. At age 14, while going over the Kuznetsky Bridge, Scriabin was knocked down by an open cab *(droshky)* and broke his right clavicle [Eaglefield Hull, 1916b; Witztum and Lerner, 2015]. At 20, in May 1893, a competitive rivalry with his contemporary piano virtuoso Josef A. Lhévinne (1874–1944), prompted by not wanting anyone to play faster and louder than he could, caused Scriabin to intensively overpractise Balakirev's Fantasy *Islamey* and Liszt's Fantasy *Don Juan*, resulting in tendonitis in his right hand, which spread up his arm; it took him two years to fully recover, during which time (1894) he composed the *Prélude et Nocturne pour la main gauche*, op. 9 [Drozdov et al., 2008; Edel, 1994].

Scriabin was not the only victim of Balakirev's

Islamey. A short few years earlier, the oriental fantasy had claimed toll on another pianist-composer: one evening in the 1880s, towards the end of a piano recital and in the middle of a performance of *Islamey*, the power of the musculature of Moritz Moszkowski (1854–1925) stopped, and his fingers, perfect masters only a moment ago, left the keys as if paralyzed [Pollack, 1925]. That medical problem with Moszkowski's arm curtailed his career as a pianist, becoming increasingly devoted to composition [Triarhou, 2011].

As his right hand became unusable, a period of frightened panic followed, his existence being in the utmost peril. If the doctors were to be believed, the impediment would have been insuparable. Nonetheless, the prognosis proved incorrect, and the complaints gradually eased off, to a large extent owing to Scriabin's will and persistence. Dwelling on the *First Sonata* in F minor, op. 6, the young Scriabin made the following inscription in his diary, an inscription that reveals the psychological stimuli of the tragic concept of the work: "At the age of 20: a serious affliction of the hand...Fate sends me an obstacle on the road to reaching brilliance and fame, my much desired goal...The first serious misfortune in my life. My first serious contemplation marks the beginning of analysis. I hope I shall get well, but my mood is very gloomy...I grumble at fate and God. I am writing the 1st Sonata with a funeral march" [Delson, 1971].

In the 1890s Scriabin also suffered from symptoms of fatigue and headaches, for which he sought treatment from the pioneer German neurologist Wilhelm H. Erb (1840–1921) of the Universities of Leipzig and Heidelberg (figure 2) [de Schloezer, 1987; Garcia, 2004]. Erb shared a deep interest in electrotherapy and promoted its rise in neurology. He had attempted to treat muscular atrophies and nervous diseases with faradisation or galvanisation as early as 1862 [Steinberg and Wagner, 2013]. He applied it as basic therapy for a host of brain disorders, including cerebral hemiplegia, bulbar palsy, partial paralysis, vertigo, headache, tinnitus, insomnia, tabes dorsalis, meningitis and myelitic processes, spinal poliomyelitis, progressive myoatrophy, paralysis in the external eye muscles, nervous ear diseases, neuralgia, migraine, and as a causal treatment for paralyses, e.g. cerebral, spinal, neuritis, or traumatic and rheumatic diseases of peripheral nerves (Steinberg,

2011).

Figure 2 Neurologists Wilhelm Erb, left, and Siegfried Bettmann, right, at Heidelberg University Clinic. Credit: Universitätsklinikum Heidelberg [Tuffs, 2008].

Scriabin was seen by Erb at the University of Heidelberg on 16 May 1895 [Altenmüller, 2015; Witztum and Lerner, 2015], at the suggestion of Belaïeff. Altschuler writes that the somber-faced youth drank all kinds of medicines, in increasingly larger doses, and seemed to be enjoying himself most when he believed his health to be the worst [Altschuler, 1972]. Such consumption of medicines would most likely be related to Scriabin's arm injuries and migraines.

In 1897 Scriabin married Vera Ivanovna Isakovich (1875–1920). In spring 1904 he stayed near Geneva, Switzerland. In summer 1905 he separated from his wife and moved near Genoa, Italy, with his formed pupil Tatyana Fyodorovna de Schloezer (1883–1922), who became his constant companion.

Scriabin had four children with his first wife, Vera. Their son Lev died in 1910, while his daughter Rimma, who was his favourite child, had died in 1906, between the Fourth Piano Sonata (1903) and *Le poème de l'extase* (1907); upon the death of eight-year-old Rimma, Scriabin composed his *Prelude* in A minor, op. 51, no. 2. He entitled it 'The broken strings' and commented, "Only he is strong and mighty, who has experienced despair and conquered it!" [Shaborkina, 1982].

With his second companion, Tatyana, Scriabin had two daughters and a son, Julian Alexandrovich in the middle, born in 1908, who accidentally drowned in the summer of 1919 while swimming in the Dnieper River; the young boy was already a composer of remarkable *Preludes* for the piano [Rodgers, 1983], having inherited both his father's genius and physical resemblance; his piano teacher had been Reinhold Glière (1875– 1956) of the Kiev Conservatory [de Schloezer, 1987]. Ariadna perished in the Resistance during the German Occupation. Marina later emigrated to Paris.

Thanks to the support of the publisher Mitrofan P. Belaïeff (1836–1904) in Leipzig, the most committed promoter of Russian music at the time, who saw into the composer's utter genius, Scriabin was able to advertise his skills abroad. Accompanied by Belaïeff, he made his first extensive tour as a pianist in 1895 visiting Germany, Holland, Belgium, Paris, Switzerland and Italy. In winter 1906, at the invitation of the conductor Modest I. Altschuler (1873–1963), an old friend from their youth years at the Moscow Conservatory, travelled to the United States, performing his Piano Concerto in New York City and giving piano recitals in Chicago, Boston, and Detroit.

The titanic workings of Scriabin's thought, his reflections, attest to him being no out-of-touch philosopher; because of his premature death, we are not justified in taking the liberty evaluating his entire philosophy, as important things were left uncompleted, not carrying out what he had in mind [Shukow, 1999]. Scriabin's attempt to embrace all branches of human knowledge led him to sink deeper into psychology, philosophical discourse, and the ambience of Ancient Hindu culture (but "not interested in modern Indians imitating the English" [Bowers, 1972]!). Thoughout his life, he was constantly immersed in philosophical speculation. He became a member of the Moscow Philosophical Society, attending its meetings regularly [de Schloezer, 1987]. In summer 1904, commuting between Vésenaz and Belotte in Switzerland, he put down extensive notes on Wundt's psychology in the same notebook in which he was drafting the first sketches of *Le poème de l'extase* [Scriabine, 1979]. At about the same time, he was contemplating *Manvatara*, the astronomical period of time measurement or one human lifespan of Manu in Hindu thought.

In September 1904 Scriabin attended the Second International Congress of Philosophy (figure 3) organised in Geneva by Édouard Claparède (figure 4, left) with speakers the calibre of Henri Bergson, Pierre Boutroux, Wincenty Lutosławski, Gaston Milhaud and Arnold Reymond [Claparède, 1905]. The Conference

Proceedings do not disclose any interaction between Scriabin and other participants. It is perhaps pertinent to note that, in the preceding three years, Claparède had published two papers on *audition colorée* ('coloured hearing') or *synopsie* (a form of synaesthesia where sounds are associated with a colour or hear in colour), in which he had argued that the colour representations that are cogitated by the auditory-colourists proper, in the majority of cases, have nothing of an object and are not the result of a logical association of ideas; he brought up the role of suggestion in the production of the phenomenon and differentiated between those who experience true colours and those who simulate seeing them [Claparède, 1900]. Claparède also had an interest in the association of colours with historical periods or the days of the week and the influence of mental life and emotional state on such colourings. Based on an experiment in two children, sister and brother, he concluded that coloured audition is not a superficial and light connection of images, but the result of a privileged association or an affective liaison [Claparède, 1903].

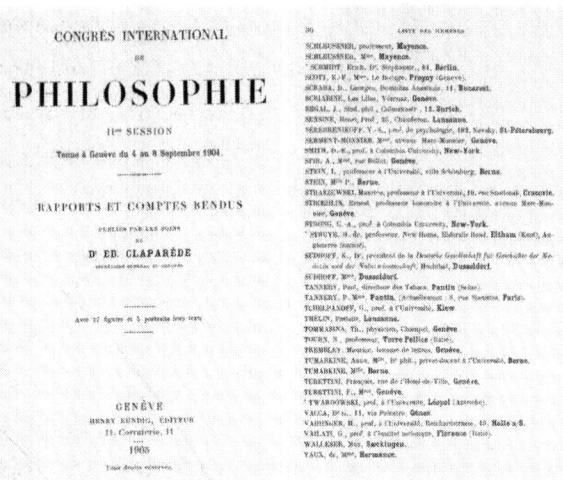

Figure 3 The cover of the *Reports and Proceedings* of the Second International Congress of Philosophy held in Geneva, and the page showing Scriabin's name (French spelling) in the roster of members. The theologian and philosopher Ernest Naville (1816–1909) was the President of Honour of the Congress. Author's archive.

Claparède is also the developer of the 'Test of Memory for Words,' the antecedent of the auditory verbal learning tests (AVLT), which has survived in modified form for 80 years [Boake, 2000]. Claparède's pioneering contributions to neuropsychology include the forensic assessment of cognitive deficits and research on implicit learning in amnesia. Moreover, he introduced the notions of 'implicit' and 'explicit' into the study of memory, described the two implicit-memory phenomena which are today called 'priming effects' and 'skill learning', and showed the influence of implicit and explicit memories in recognition. His approach places him among the most important precursors of the theories of human memory [Eustache et al., 1996].

Figure 4 Left, the Swiss neurologist-psychologist Édouard Claparède, M.D. (1873–1940), nephew of the comparative anatomist René-Édouard Claparède (1832–1871). Right, the British physician-psychologist Charles S. Myers, M.D., F.R.S., C.B.E. (1873–1946). The two gentlemen were born 11 days apart, the year after Scriabin was born. Claparède completed his thesis on the muscular sense in cases of posthemiplegic ataxia in 1897 and Myers on myasthenia gravis in 1901. Portrait credits: Notre Histoire/Université de Genève, Switzerland (left); National Portrait Gallery, London (right).

The orchestral work *Le poème de l'Extase* (1905–1908) was written in Switzerland after the *Third Symphony*. It was initially conceived as a 'Fourth Symphony,' titled *Poème orgiaque* (stemming from Scriabin's interest in Dionysian mysteries [Bowers, 1972]).

In 1908 Scriabin 'discovered' the book *La clef de la Théosophie* ('The key to Theosophy') by Madame Helena P. Blavatsky, the occultist who had co-founded the Theosophical Society in New York in 1875. He read it and found it "the most extraordinary book" [Bowers, 1972]. What further had an effect on Scriabin were discussions with Prince Sergei N. Trubetskoy (1863–1905), a religious philosopher whose father was the co-founder of Moscow Conservatory in 1866 with Anton Rubinstein's brother. Nevertheless, Scriabin rejected some of Trubetskoy's spiritual and idealistic disciplines that dominated society, regarding them as obstacles on his own path [de Schloezer, 1987]. Although the two eccentrics, Blavatsky and Trubetskoy, led Scriabin's thinking into evermore recondite fields [Mann, 1980], he used theosophical terms quite loosely, adapting them to his personal ideas, aspirations and yearnings [de Schloezer, 1987].

As he dabbled into mystical philosophy, he became as well interested in the relationship of sound and tonality to colour; his musical language entered a new phase and led to his subsequent symphonic works, such as *Le poème de l'extase* and *Le poème du feu* [Sabaneiev, 1974]. In Scriabin's own words, "Through music and colour, with the aid of perfume, the human mind or soul can be lifted outside or above merely physical sensations into the region of purely abstract ecstasy and purely intellectual speculation." The mystic Scriabin admits that in his speculations he relies wholly on his intuitions, science as yet having uttered no word [Runciman, 1915]. He has been defined as a solipsist, adhering to the philosophical idea that only the knowledge of self is possible, and for each individual, mind itself is the only thing sure to exist [Bowers, 1972].

In his travels to Europe and America as a soloist and virtuoso of the first order, Scriabin performed exclusively his own compositions. He had made it a principle very early on to interpret nothing but his own compositions. Without ambiguity, he declared: "I play only Scriabin," and took pleasure in playing his works. He showed pettiness when analysing the music of someone else [de Schloezer, 1987], and even ended his friendship with pianist Arthur Rubinstein when the latter confessed that he liked the music of Brahms very much [Bowers, 1972]. Scriabin recorded some of his piano pieces on cylinders and rolls with the Hupfeld Company on the *Phonola* (1912) and *Welte-Mignon* (1913) apparatus, in vehement interpretations with solid dynamic construction and technical precision [Franke, 1973; Lischke, 1997].

Regarding physique, Scriabin was described as "an unusual, somber-faced youth, slight of build, immaculate of dress, patronising of air; he wore a small, pointed beard, but is was the eyes, seemingly a changeable green, that captured one, with an expression ever watchful, enigmatic, inscrutable. In a characteristic gesture of his small and delicate hands, he tapped the left hand with the fingers of his right" [Altschuler, 1972]. Socially, he had few friends, but accepted them with full affection [Altschuler, 1972]. Regarding mentality, Scriabin's enemies said he was insane, whereas his friends said he was just smarter that the rest of us [Bowers, 1972]. Scriabin greatly prized the works of Aeschylus and interpreted *Prometheus* as the disobedient venturer who, besides bearing fire to humans literally speaking, also presented them with the fire of intelligence, enabling them to be superior to God [Bowers, 1972]. He had absolute faith in the unlimited power of human free will [de Schloezer, 1987]. He uttered that the artist is more important than God and that politicians and bureaucrats are not to be praised. "Writers, composers, authors and sculptors are the first-ranking in the Universe, first to expound principles and doctrines, and to solve world problems. Real progress rests on artists alone. They must not give place to others of lower aims" [Bowers, 1972; Garcia, 2004]. He also submitted that "A God who needs adoration, is not God" [Scriabine, 1979].

On 1 February 1913 the English première of *Prometheus* took place at Queen's Hall. The work was performed twice, in both halves of the concert: in the first part of the programme it was preceded by Haydn's *Symphony* No. 98, and in the second half of the programme by Beethoven's *Violin Concerto* [Rudakova and Kandinsky, 1980]. In 1914 Scriabin journeyed to London for a performance of his *Piano Concerto* and of *Prométhée* under the conductor Sir Henry J. Wood. On

20 and 26 March 1914 Scriabin concertised solo with recitals of his own compositions at the Bechstein Hall, London, where he was very favourably received. Apparently, one of his motives for travelling to London was to meet the woman in whose arms Blavatsky had died [Bowers, 1972].

In early 1914 Scriabin wrote *K plyameni* ('Vers la flamme') before returning to London. In the summer he finished his last works and laboured over the text of the *Predvaritelnoye deystvo*. Back in Moscow he gave a number of concerts with works from every stage in his life, ranging from *Valse*, op. 1 to some of the *Preludes*, op. 74. Scriabin's last public performance was on 15 April 1915 in Saint Petersburg, after three piano recitals there [de Schloezer, 1987]. The praise from the press reached new heights.

During his tournée, he noticed a carbuncle below his moustache on his upper lip, reminiscent of the one which had afflicted him in London a year earlier. By 20 April he was bedridden and his temperature rose rapidly. His doctors opened it; one incision by his physicians was followed by others, but by then two types of generalised septicaemia had set in. By 24 April crowds thronged the staircase of his flat — the situation had become grave. As he lay dying, he mourned, "This means the end, but what a catastrophe!" [Hope, 1970]. Scriabin died at 8 a.m. on 27 April 1915 at the age of 43, with the manuscript containing sketches for the *Misteriya* open on his piano [Powell, 2000]. Death came to Scriabin at a time when he had been writing about death as apotheosis for his *Prefatory Act* ("A sacred instant of creation, fiery instant…the reflection—pale, white and fatal—of Death") [Garcia, 2004]. Such a large crowed of people attended the funeral of their hero that tickets had to be issued. Scriabin was interred at the Cemetery of Novodevichy Monastery in Moscow.

Scriabin died poor and left his first wife Vera, his companion Tatyana, and his children penniless. The following year, his former classmate Rachmaninoff did a grand tour with all Scriabin programmes up and down the Volga and turned all the revenue to Tatyana. This was the first time that Rachmaninoff ever performed in public compositions other than his own, and it was those recitals that started his career as a concert pianist [Bowers, 1972].

Legacy

Scriabin was born on Christmas 1871 according to the old Russian calendar (or Theophany 1872 according to the Gregorian calendar). This may be one of the reasons why the composer saw himself as a messianic apostle of divine art in the cause of human emancipation, at the same time juxtaposing the preaching of Christ to the act of Prometheus, the Aeschylean demigod [Rüger, 1980]. It is infrequently mentioned that Scriabin died on Good Friday. That is imprecise. Perhaps it stems from Gorenstein's fiction novel [Gorenstein, 1992]. In 1915, Russian Orthodox Easter Sunday was on 4 April (22 March in the old-style Julian Calendar). Scriabin died 25 days after Good Friday 1915. Shortly after his death, Scriabin was declared by the Russian composer Yevgeny Gunst (1877–1950), in one of the earliest biographies, "the greatest genius of the 20th century" with a significance equal to that of Bach, Beethoven, Chopin and Wagner [Gunst, 1915]. Eaglefield Hull [1916b] was convinced in 1916 that the *Ten Sonatas* are destined in the future to occupy a niche of their own, alongside the 48 *Preludes and Fugues* of

Bach, the 32 *Sonatas* of Beethoven, the pianoforte works of Brahms, and the music of Chopin.

Decades after being a *persona non grata* in the eyes of the Soviet regime, Scriabin became a "mascot" of the cosmonaut programme, fueling the national pride: during the historic 1 h 48 min first manned spaceflight by Yuri Gagarin around the Earth on 12 April 1961, Soviet Radio beamed *Le poème de l'extase* into Gagarin's spacecraft, a fitting choice for an event of such stratospheric heights. Three days later, upon Gagarin's return to the Red Square, Scriabin's music again complemented the triumphant mood, with the *Second Symphony* performed during the celebrations [Ballard, 2010].

On 6 January 1972 a special committee, under composer Rodion Shchedrin, opened the Scriabin centennial celebrations in the Grand Hall of the Moscow Conservatory, which did much to highlight the never-dwindling importance of Scriabin's work [Rudakova and Kandinsky, 1984]. That year, the Soviet Union issued a Scriabin centennial stamp (Scott 3938). The *Melodiya* Gramophone Record Firm released from their archives a commemorative set of two LP records

(GOST 5289-68) in 1972 with works by Scriabin recorded by his son-in-law Vladimir Sofronitsky (1901– 1961) on the centennial of the composer's birth, and another commemorative set of two LP records (R10 01071–01074) in 1992 with historic performances (1910–1986) of Scriabin pieces played by Scriabin, Rachmaninoff, Prokofiev, Goldenweiser, Feinberg, Sofronitsky, Neuhaus and Horowitz on the occasion of the 120th Anniversary of his birth. In 1997, the Russian Federation issued a two-ruble silver coin (Krause Y550) for Scriabin's 125th birthday. The flat where Scriabin lived from October 1912 until April 1915 in Moscow is now the Scriabin State Museum.

The pianist Nikita Magaloff, acquainted with Scriabin's compositions since his early childhood, spoke about his singular nature, unmistakeable difference, liberation from 'local' influences, and placement as an indispensable monument in the pantheon of pianistic writing; according to this master, "Scriabin is really a special case; his apparition on the scene is as inexplicable as the fleeing yet unbroken nature of his evolution, somewhat like Beethoven" [Rist, 1994]. When we recognise how far beyond his predecessors he was able to go with how little new machinery, we then begin to realise his significance and his position, certainly individual and at present unique among the composers of the last three centuries [Antcliffe, 1924].

Pianist Igor Zhukov, one of the most deeply versed Scriabinians, refutes, as the composer did, the theories that purported to prove that the source of the Scriabin phenomenon was to be traced to the musical models set by Chopin, Liszt and Wagner [Shukow, 1999]. Rather, Zhukov explains that, in his mysterious and majestic temple, that singular structure in the musical culture of the world, Scriabin followed no one and left no one to follow him, leaning towards creative independence and freedom; in the brief 25 years of his creative life he evolved like a spiral whose first whorl was rooted in the late romantic period and whose last whorl reached out to contemporary musical idiom and ideology. Thanks to his fantasy and quest for beauty, he "penetrated distant worlds and touched upon cosmic mysteries." Scriabin meant 'creation' as a *Triad* that comprised: an unremitting desire, an unlimited capacity for enthusiasm, and a purpose or determination, which the person must continually advance and enrich.

Scriabin's style

Scriabin's complex harmonic theory was extremely systematic and disciplined. Departing from the major-minor context of classical harmony, he invented something new and unique, "a total entity within itself," according to Bower, levelling the vertical and horizontal differences between harmony and melody to a single unit of compression [Mackey, 1994]. Scriabin actually considered "melody to be harmony in horizontal form and harmony to be melody in vertical form" and that "melody is harmony unfurled, harmony is furled melody" [Bowers, 1969]. Despite Scriabin's view that harmony and melody are one and the same, often the vertical and horizontal aspects of his music are discussed separately.

The preoccupation of some modern writers with Scriabin's theories and eroticism seems to be only a reflection of their own misplaced onanistic exhibitionism. By mixing pseudo-psychoanalytical jargon with word-game banters, somehow, they unwittingly force the music into second place. What is true and what is important is that Scriabin was a man ahead of his time, one of

Music's real innovators, who left a magnificent legacy of beauty. Scriabin did not just imitate Chopin: he developed an unmatched, uncanny style of his own [Garvelmann, 1982].

Scriabin's works are like polished diamonds that lie cool in one's hand, yet radiate iridescent fire, bundled energy, flickering light, in a boundless rapture of beauty [van den Hoogen, 1979]. Every work of his, even the smallest, is a multifaceted crystal in which, merged into one, are the powerful breath of nature, and the strong thinking, imagination and deep soul of the artist; to him, the piano was a living being, with whom he shared his thoughts and feelings [Shaborkina, 1980].

In his planned artistic affranchisement, he anticipated the multimedia aspects so fashionable in today's art world [Cohn, 1968]. He developed a "mystic chord," an arrangement in fourths rather than thirds, which, with its transpositions and contrapuntal elements, led to the very door of atonality and polytonality, prefiguring Schoenberg's dodecaphony. In his last compositions, such as *Guirlandes*, Op. 73, the tonal passions of Scriabin are like the concatenations of a musical Proust.

Scriabin's work is one of the most original of all music; totally revolutionary, of no less caliber than that of Schoenberg, Bartók, Prokofiev or Stravinsky, jostling tonality in an irreversibly manner, inventing, like Chopin, his own forms, developing an aesthetics of miniature in a straight line with the attempts of the latter Liszt, mastering harmonic horizons and unusual sonorous spaces which Messiaen will recall, to say nothing of Berg, Szymanowski or more modern composers, such as Stockhausen and Cage, Scriabin put to music questions that had not been put before him. Creator at the jostling transition of worlds between the nineteenth and the twentieth centuries, divided between total romanticism and radical modernism, absolute mystic and prophet of a new world, Scriabin made of art a sort of religion and of magical initiation appealing to transform life. One hundred years after his death, he is more than ever our contemporary [Clément, 2015].

OMNI-ART

Prometheus, opus 60

SCRIABIN'S LATER WORKS reveal an outright disregard for the 'theoretical foundations of musical art' [Gunst, 1915]. He founded a new chord by selecting the sounds he prefers from Nature's harmonic chord and building them up by fourths. The result is a chord of extreme interest and beauty. He adopts the system wholeheartedly and all that it involves, a veritable revolution in music that abolishes major and minor modes, dispenses with key-signatures, and fully accepts the equal temperament in tuning [Eaglefield Hull, 1916a]. The two orchestral works, in which Scriabin deliberately associates music with colours, spring from his 'final period' and are *Prometheus* and the unfinished *Mysterium*.

Prométhée: Le poème du feu, op. 60 (1909–1910) or

Scriabin's 'Fifth Symphony,' his last completed symphonic work, presents a complex program, which concludes with the beginnings of the Cosmos and a cosmic dance of the atoms. *Prometheus* is a hybrid [40] between a symphonic poem, a concealed piano concerto, a sonata augmented by an introduction and a coda, and a 'multimedia' cantata for four-part wordless chorus and full-scale orchestra, amplified by extra strings and winds (eight horns and five trumpets), a keyboard called *Svetovaya klaviatura* or *Tastiera per luce*, which makes no sound but produces colours, piano, organ, bells, glockenspiel, celesta, and two harps. In his opus 60 Scriabin made his first true attempt to systematically connect music with colours (see coloured scale on rear cover of the book).

In 1916 Sabaneiev published an exhaustive commentary on the relationship of colour and sound in the score of *Prometheus*. Yet the meaning of Scriabin's art can be fully understood only in terms of general culture [de Schloezer, 1987].

Scriabin's 'central sound' for horizontal harmonies and vertical melodies ("...we face an ecumenical consciousness that experiences a plethora of conscious

states vertically in time and horizontally in space...")
developed from a layering of thirds on the dominant to
a stack of fourths. The six-note chord, which opens the
work as a symbol of the all-embracing primordial
chaos, the 'Promethean chord,' is schematically struc-
tured in augmented, pure and diminished fourths: A –
D-sharp – G – C-sharp – F-sharp – B (colours: blue-
violet-grey). A 'mystic chord' of fourths (C – F-sharp –
B-flat – E – A – D) also appears in the middle of the
Fifth Sonata for piano. The corpus of *Prometheus* be-
gins with the 'Theme of Understanding' (brilliant blue
colour), played on the piano. The development theme
is built on red hues. Following a whirling cosmic dance
(dans un vertige), the work culminates with the 'Promethean chord' clarified in F-sharp major (blue colour). The idea of the composer was to fill the whole hall
with blinding rays as the full forces of orchestra and
chorus are mobilised, with the main theme played by
the five trumpets against organ harmonies; after a sud-
den silence, a lilac twilight of an intoxicating dance, piano and cymbal passages, a sea of sounds from the orchestra merge in the final chord, which is the only
'triad' that the composer uses in the entire work [Sa-

baneiev, 1974].

The evolution and audacity of Scriabin's harmonies in his final works, including *Prometheus*, can be traced, from his earliest works such as the *Valse*, op. 1, to the *Second* and *Third Symphony* and the *Preludes*, op. 37 [Sabaneiev, 1974]. In particular, the programme of the *Fourth Sonata*, op. 30 (1903) for piano seems to be *Prometheus*'s essence, out of which develop all the cosmic conceptions which followed; the *Seventh Sonata*, op. 64 (1912), the 'White Mass' that followed *Prometheus* is also related to the *Poem of Fire*: "The Universe is in flames, the spirit achieves the peak of existence" [Shukow, 1999].

Scriabin had originally planned to bring in the use of light in *Le poème de l'extase*, op. 54. Eventually, he included it in the score of *Le poème du feu*, op. 60: the two top staves in *Prometheus* contain two *Luce* parts for the visual effects: the upper stave follows the course of the harmony, while the lower stave moves independently through the visible spectrum [40]. If tones are arranged on the circle of fifths, then a regularity of colours becomes obvious, where they arrange themselves almost exactly according to the spectrum [Sabaneiev, 1974].

One reason for including light elements in the *Poem of Fire* could be fire itself, which occupied a central position in Russian culture both for its comforting value in the cold winters and for its destructive force. Further, Scriabin had thouroughly studied Aeschylus' Trilogy of *Prometheus* (chained on the Caucasus) and Dante's Divine Comedy (and purgatories). Stravinsky had just composed his *Feu d'artifice* ('Fireworks', 1908) and *L'oiseau de feu* ('Firebird', 1910).

Flames make the subject of two of Scriabin's last three published compositions, *Vers la flamme*, op. 72, and *Deux danses (Guirlandes, Flammes sombres)*, op. 73. In the piano poem *Vers la flamme*, op. 72, composed just before the outbreak of the First World War in 1914, the melody consists mostly of descending half-steps with unusual harmonies and tremolos that create an intense, fiery luminance. According to Vladimir Horowitz, the piece was inspired by Scriabin's conviction that a constant accumulation of heat would ultimately cause the destruction of the world. The title reflects the fiery destruction of the Earth, and the constant emotional crescendo leads, ultimately, "Toward the flame." This poem is one of the most important of all Scriabin's pieces; advanced in harmony, it is thoroughly radiant and luminous. In colour and mood, as well as in its triumphant ending it is closely allied to *Prometheus* [Eaglefield Hull, 1916b] and has much the same psychological basis as *Prometheus* [Antcliffe, 1924].

Two Dances, op. 73, resemble each other like brother and sister. No. 1, titled *Guirlandes*, is a passage from the *Mysterium*, where he evokes flowers, dancers waving garlands in the air. No. 2, *Flammes sombres* ('Dark flames') its contrasting mate, is subdued, somber and thoughful. Its lambent colours are embers, even during the middle section where you can feel dancers' skirts swirling around a fire. The fire here is dark, dark as the music's mood. He often said, "You hear, this is not music any longer…it is something else…It is the *Mysterium*" [Bowers, 1969]. These two dances have strong mystic elements which render the meaning very obscure [Eaglefield Hull, 1916b].

One of the earliest biographies of Scriabin, authored by the distinguished Oxford scholar and organist Arthur Eaglefield Hull, Mus.D. (1876–1928), was published the year after the composer's death [Eaglefield

Hull, 1916b]. Hull devotes an entire chapter to 'Music and Colour' where he approaches the analogy between colour and sound and the manner of applying the scale of colours to the musical scale from the viewpoint of inventors and philosophers. He discusses the "colour organ" invented and used in June 1895 by the British painter Alexander W. Rimington, A.R.E., R.B.A. (1854–1918), Professor of Fine Arts at Queen's College [Rimington, 1912]. Hull makes a distinction as far as the elements in music that serve the purpose of colour, distinguishing between orchestral timbre (or tone-colour) and chromatic harmony. According to Hull, Scriabin adopted Rimington's colour-keyboard for *Prometheus* ("a dual Symphony of Sound and Colour—two Symphonies at once in fact"), but used a Colour Scale of his own, founded on the piano-tuner's "cycle of fifths," and wrote music in a novel harmonic and scientific system to give the colour-symphony a fair opportunity of making its effect. Scriabin placed twelve hues on a small 12-note keyboard, with the colour harmonies following more or less closely the bass notes of his novel harmonies. The sentence that comes closest to relating colour and music on mental lines and the effect that such relation produces on the mind is that "Scriabin's evident preference for the key of F-sharp major seems to point to some connection of this sort in his mind."

When *son et lumières* are combined, one of the modern artists that come to mind is the French composer Jean-Michel Jarre, known for organising outdoor spectacles of music with features of lights, laser displays, and fireworks. Three years after the release of *Oxygène*, the "magician of sound" became the "magician of light" when, in 1979, Jarre and his producer Francis Dreyfus proposed an experimental concert at Place de la Concorde in Paris, combining music, light and pyrotechnics, which attracted an unprecedented crowd of one million and gave birth to the concept of 'Cities in concert' —including Lyon, Houston, London and Moscow, with millions of people dreaming awake before the audio-visual prowess of Jarre's spectacles [Duguay, 2011].

The March 1911 premières at Moscow and Saint Petersburg under S. Koussevitsky, with Scriabin playing the solo part on the piano, did not include the colour keyboard, owing to a technical problem [Skans, 1991]. The American première, which was the first performance with light, took place on 20 March 1915 in Carnegie Hall (actually performed twice, with a brief intermission) under Modest Altschuler, with the *Tastiera per luce* and with the colour effects developed by the Electrical Testing Laboratories; the lighting instrument used was the *chromola*, which resembled Rimington's "colour keyboard" but was engineered by Preston S. Millar.

Sound and light performances resumed later, with concerts in 1962 in Kazan, U.S.S.R. by the *Prometei* group of artists and engineers [Galeyev and Vanechkina, 2001], at Yale University in 1969 with even clouds of incense pumped from air ducts, and again in 2010 thanks to an initiative by Gawboy and Townsend [2012], in 1970 on the Southern Illinois University campus by the St. Louis Symphony Orchestra under Walter Susskind [Hope, 1970], in 1992 by the Berlin Philharmonic under Claudio Abbado with pianist Martha Argerich, in 2009 at the Ice Palace of Saint Petersburg, Russia, and in 2013 in Tokyo by the NHK Symphony under Vladimir Ashkenazy with pianist Peter Jablonski, to name a few.

The unfinished Mysterium

Prometheus gives us only an impression of what was prevented by Scriabin's premature death: the conceived masterpiece *Mysterium*, which would present a theosophical interpretation of the evolutionary psychology of humanity, right up to its purifying ecstasy and cosmic freedom [Rüger, 1980; de Schloezer, 1987].

The key to Scriabin's creative personality, the project that circumscribed his entire career, musical and philosophical, was the 'Ultimate Act' that would culminate in an ecstatic union with the supernal Unique Being [Scriabine, 1987]. In the early period of Scriabin's life, the *Mysterium* did not exist as a concept. Nonetheless, all his creations are approximations gradually leading to the *Mysterium*, the dream of unifying humanity in a common beatitude of ecstasy which would transfigure and deify humans and the Universe and would lead to a new Cosmos [de Schloezer, 1987].

By 'Mystery' Scriabin did not mean anything baffling or misunderstood, as in *misterioso*. He meant it in the sense of the Dionysian and the Eleusinian mysteries, and also in the Christian sense, enacted in temples and cathedrals [Bowers, 1972]. It was to be a liturgical drama that would effect a synthesis of all the arts to the end of preparing the way for consummation [de Schloezer, 1987].

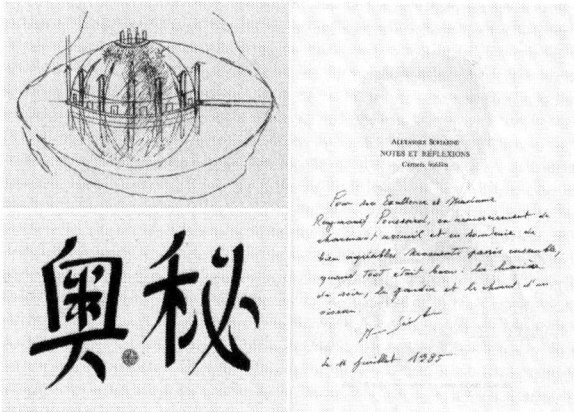

Figure 5 Upper left, a sketch by Scriabin of the temple where the *Mystère* was to be celebrated [Scriabine, 1979]. It does not bear any inscription, but Scriabin had talked about it to Boris de Schloezer. The edifice, in the shape of a semi-dome, would be elevated over the water plane in the middle of a lake, such that, by its reflection, it would appear as a perfect sphere; colour shafts of light would give the impression of a varying architecture. It is difficult to specify any further details. One notices six portals (thus twelve in total), and a crown of stars near the crown. The meaning and function of the 'pillars' is elusive. Lower left, *Mystère*, calligraphie chinoise by Su Ting, Grenoble. Right, autograph dedication of the French edition of Scriabin's 'Notes and Reflections' [Scriabine, 1979] by his daughter Marina, dated 16 July 1985; Marina Scriabin studied decorative arts and music in Paris and obtained a Doctorate in Aesthetics. Author's archive.

Scriabin loosely formulated the idea of *Mysterium* around late 1902 or early 1903 [de Schloezer, 1987; Macdonald, 1999]. In his library he kept texts and poetical works, such as Sophocles' *Tragedies*, in the translation of Tadeusz S. Zieliński (1859–1944), and Plato's *Symposium*, in the translation of Vladimir S. Solovyov (1853–1900), to help himself with the theatrical aspect of the *Acte préalable* (*Predvaritelnoye Deistvo*, 'Prefatory Act'), which he began drafting in 1913 [Bowers, 1969; de Schloezer, 1987]. He read after supper. Inspired by musical innovation, his philosophical and theosophical pursuits, and oriental mysticism, the work would prepare humans for the celebration of *Mysterium*, which would for the first time reveal a 'total art,' a radically new aesthetic language including what Scriabin felt was most likely an intended unification of music, coloured lights, mist, incenses and fragrances, drama, poetry, dance, in his quest for an integration that would encompass all human senses, creating a synthesis of the acoustic, the optical, the choreographic and the plastic. It would be performed against the backdrop of the Himalayas (figure 5) as an "immense liturgical rite" repeated over seven days and seven nights and elevating humankind to a higher world [Witztum and Lerner, 2015]. Spectators would be participants in an "oneness" of performers and audience.

Scriabin desired the renowned bass Feodor I. Chaliapin (1873–1938) to sing, prima ballerina Tamara P. Karsavina (1885–1978) to dance, and theatrical director Alexander Y. Tairov (1885–1950) to set the stage [Bowers, 1972].

When the First World War broke out in 1914, Scriabin was at work on the text of *Acte préalable* (it was published posthumously in 1919 in Berlin, in the Russian gazette *Les Propylées*). He had conceived the idea of composing a Preliminary Act, which would serve as the threshold to the *Mysterium* or a species of initiation, the previous year. During winter 1914–1915 he often played sections from the unfinished music to *Acte préalable* for Tatyana's brother Boris, revealing visions of the future *Mysterium*, and occasionally giving signs that he was then already removed from earthly life [de Schloezer, 1987]. His last opus, *Five Preludes*, op. 74, contains a distant echo of *Acte*.

Scriabin's ultimate inspiration was to effect a unified art form that comprised all sensory modalities. He used to say, "I shall not die, I shall suffocate in ecstasy after the *Mysterium*" [Hope, 1970]. Scriabin dedicated the final phase of his life to his "ultimate work" studying Sanskrit, taking yoga breathing exercises and purchasing a plot of land in Darjeeling. What animates the artistic desing of *Mysterium* is both the synthesis of all arts and the inclusion in the sphere of art of elements even outside the field of aesthetics [de Schloezer, 1987]. The idea of a unity of all arts — the basis of the doctrine of an Omni-art — arose from Scriabin's intuitive experience as, to him, sound had no separate existence from colours, images or concepts.

The Russian composer Alexander Nemtin (1936–1999) worked on reconstructing the *Mysterium* over two decades from 30 extant poetic text pages and 53 pages of musical score fragments of themes and harmonies by Scriabin; Nemtin called the first part *Universe* [Makarova-Nemtin and Portugalov, 1999]. It premiered in Moscow on 16 March 1973 by the Moscow Philharmonic Orchestra under Kirill Kondrashin and released 20 years later under the Russian Disc label (CD 11004) [Ledin and Ledin, 1993]. The *Univers (Cosmogonie) – Humanité – Transfiguration* trilogy, re-

alised by Nemtin, was recorded by the Deutsches Sym-
phonie-Orchester Berlin under Vladimir Ashkenazy
between September 1996 and August 1997 and released
in 1999 under the Decca Record Company label (3CD
289 466 329-2). In both recordings the pianist is Alexei
Lubimov.

TESTIMONIES

THE EXACT WAY the two authors of the essential primary biographies and closest Scriabin confidants express his music-colour association is as follows.

His brother-in-law Boris F. de Schloezer (1881–1969), in a first-hand account of the composer's spiritual and artistic development, originally published in 1923 by the Russian émigré press *Grani* in Berlin, writes [de Schloezer, 1987]: "Scriabin possessed a special sense of colour in musical sounds. In his desire to invest musical images with verbal ideas, he dreamt of symphonies of odours and tastes...To Scriabin the music of *Prometheus* radiated light and scintillated colours; he remarked that violet light should permeate the concert hall in the opening bars and that the 'Promethean chord' represented to his mind both a sound and a tone, a sound-colour, not a sound accompanied by violet or any other light. This grandiose conception, portending a synthesis of all the arts, can be understood only by taking into consideration the idiosyncratic traits of Scriabin's personality…Scriabin's synthesis of the arts was based on the idea of an intimate intermingling of all artistic disciplines, and their essential oneness in an all-embracing Omni-art. He called this process 'counterpoint,' as opposed to Wagner's parallelism of music and drama. Scriabin's method was the result of his musical philosophy."

The musicologist Leonid L. Sabaneiev (1881–1968), also physicist and mathematician, qualifies that association as "A. N. Scriabin's intuition of colour-sounds" [Sabaneiev, 1974]. Sabaneiev had studied at the Moscow Conservatory under Rimsky-Korsakov, Taneyev, Zverev, and Boris de Schloezer's uncle Pavel Y. de Schloezer (1841–1898) and later transcribed *Prometheus* for two pianos. He explains that what Scriabin attempts to do in *Prometheus* is unite music with one of the "accompanying" arts, i.e. the play of colours, which "indescribably strengthen the impression produced by the music."

Scriabin's daughter Marina explains, however, that

Sabaneiev was one among the many who wrote about her father who "distorted Scriabin's utterances or misinterpreted them" and that her uncle Schloezer was in all probability the only person among Scriabin's close associates capable or reporting Scriabin's ideas about art in their integrity and unity, in its totality and its place within his own individuality [Scriabine, 1987].

The Myers encounter

The most direct evidence on Scriabin's tone and colour associations derives from an interview that the composer had granted during his visit to London in 1914 to Charles S. Myers [van Campen, 2008], who recorded that interview in a published report as the first of "two cases of synaesthesia" [Myers, 1914].

Myers' interest in Scriabin had led him to London to hear the composer perform the piano part in *Prometheus* on 14 March 1914. Scriabin wrote to Tatyana Schloezer, "Tomorrow A. N. and I are driving to Cambridge where we shall spend the entire day at the invitation of two professors. They are interested in the colour symphony and my ideas in general. An interview with them should be very interesting" [Peacock, 1985].

One of the professors mentioned in the letter was Myers. The other professor was most likely Myers' collaborator, the educational psychologist Charles Wilfred Valentine, D.Phil. (1879–1964), Lecturer at University of St. Andrews at the time, who had just published a book on the psychology of beauty [Valentine, 1913] (figure 6).

Charles Samuel Myers (figure 4, right) was an English physician with a pre-eminent position in the history of British psychology. A talented violinist with diverse interests in physiology, physical and social anthropology, music appreciation, philosophy, history and the classics, and experimental psychology (the main scientific pursuit of his scientific life), he taught his students how to treat psychology as a genuine biological science without forgetting the wide human world beyond the laboratory. Myers obtained his M.D. degree in 1901 from the Gonville and Gaius College of Cambridge University; he was a founding member of the British Psychological Society (1901), in which he served as Secretary and President; started and edited the *British Journal of Psychology* (1911–1924), and built the National Institute of Industrial Psychology [Bartlett, 1948].

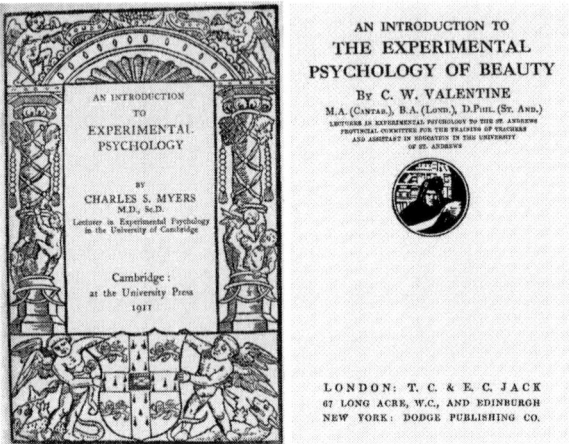

Figure 6 Title pages of the psychology textbooks by Myers [1911b] and Valentine [1913]. Credit: The Open Archive (www.archive.com).

In 1902 Myers began teaching physiology of the special senses at Cambridge; in 1909 he became the first physician whose whole duty was to teach experimental psychology. At the time when he met with Scriabin, he was Lecturer in Experimental Psychology at Cambridge and former Professor and Chair of Experimental Psychology (1906–1909) at King's College, and had published his pioneering and genuinely original 432-page

Textbook [Myers, 1909] and 156-page *Introduction* [Myers, 1911b] to experimental psychology (figure 6). In 1912, Myers established the first-class Cambridge Laboratory of Experimental Psychology, the first such in England, which he directed through 1930. His research involved the elements of rhythm and melody in ethnic music, perception, animal behaviour, the behaviour of twins, the development of colour sense, the influence of binaural phase differences on sound localisation, instinct and intelligence, synaesthesia, shell shock in battle, the nature of mind, and education. Myers was elected Fellow of the Royal Society in 1915 and was awarded the Commander of the Most Excellent Order of the British Empire (C.B.E.) in 1919.

The impediment, towards a thorough investigation, of having to communicate in French was partially alleviated by the cooperation of Alexander N. Briantschaninoff (a wealthy publisher, the A. N. that Scriabin mentions in his letter, who had planned to send Scriabin to India to become consecrated by the Mahatmas [Butler, 2013]). I next paraphrase and reiterate key fragments from the Myers study.

For Scriabin colour formed an important part of the

total sound effect. His *Prometheus* was to be performed to the accompaniment of lamps that flooded the concert hall with lights of ever-changing colours. His *Mysterium*, when completed, would be presented with similar colour plays, and with odours as well.

The attention of Scriabin was seriously drawn to his "coloured hearing" for the first time at a concert in Paris, where he was sitting next to Nikolai Rimsky-Korsakov. Scriabin remarked that a piece in D major [not specified which], that they were listening to, seemed yellow; Rimsky-Korsakov replied that, to him, the colour seemed golden. From then on, Scriabin compared with several musicians the colour effects of diverse keys. He disagreed with Rimsky-Korsakov regarding the key of F-sharp, which was perceived by the two composers as violet (A.S.) and green (N.R.K.). Scriabin rationalised that such a "deviation" could be attributed to the frequent use of that particular key in pastoral music and, therefore, to the colour of leaves and grass.

Scriabin thought that the specific colours he obtained must be shared by anyone endowed with coloured hearing. Myers argues that Scriabin's "chromaesthesia" referred to music *tonality*, rather than *pitch* or *timbre* or even the *name* of a note. Colours change with tonality, or "colour *underlines* tonality and makes it more evident." Occasionally, colour or a change of colour appeared to Scriabin *before* being aware of the tonality or of a tonality change. Scriabin thought that the simultaneous presentation of the appropriate colour to the eyes *enhanced* the musical effect.

The composer told Myers that, when listening to music, he only had a *feeling* of colour; an *image* of colour was given only in cases where the feeling was very intense. On the other hand, Scriabin noted that "older music" with its infrequent changes of tonality gave him colour changes in *intensity* rather than in *quality*, as "it had not the psychological basis of modern music." With regard to Beethoven's Symphonies, in particular, Scriabin argued that those do not need colour, because they are "too intellectual in character."

Myers concludes that "for Scriabin a single note has in itself no colour; it has the colour of its tonality." Scriabin insisted that single tones cannot occur alone, either within or outside music, since tones are always accompanied by both harmonic and inharmonic overtones in nature, in combined tonalities and thus, a con-

THE CONTRIVED
SYNAESTHESIA

Null hypothesis: the assumption

IN THE NEUROLOGICAL AND BIOMEDICAL literature phrases such as these abound: "Synaesthesia has frequently been reported among poets, novelists, artists and musicians, such as Arthur Rimbaud, Charles Baudelaire, Vassily Kandinsky, Vladimir Nabokov, Alexander Scriabin, Olivier Messiaen and David Hockney" [Kay and Mulvenna, 2006; Pollak et al., 2007]. "Scriabin, Sibelius, Rimsky-Korsakov and Messiaen were probably synaesthetes" [Warren, 1999]. "Alexander Scriabin and Nikolai Rimsky-Korsakov are believed to have had coloured-hearing synaesthesia" [Brust, 2001, 2003]. "Most of the eminent personalities who we know were definitely synaesthetic are men — the novelist Nabokov, the Russian composer Alexander Scriabin and the British artist Hockney are examples"

[Sinha, 2001]. "The list of famous figures who were involved with the synaesthetic experience includes Charles Baudelaire, Arthur Rimbaud, Nikolai Rimsky-Korsakov, Alexander Scriabin, Vassily Kandinsky, Vladimir Nabokov, Sergei Eisenstein, Olivier Messiaen, David Hockney and Richard Feynman" [Ione, 2006; Ione and Tyler, 2004].

In the musical literature it is also often taken for granted that Scriabin had synaesthesia [Baylor, 1974]: "His scores became peppered with such markings as 'Luminously and more and more flashing.' It might be that Scriabin also suffered from a rare genetic peculiarity known as synaesthesia, in which sound is translated directly into colour. People with synaesthesia cannot hear music without seeing colours" [Schonberg, 1975]. The term "synaesthesia" has often been used metaphorically rather than accurately. Ongoing scientific research shows the condition to be "real" rather than imagined. The author focuses her discussion on the effects of colour-sound synaesthesia, or "chromaesthesia," are discussed in relation to Scriabin, Olivier Messiaen and Michael Torke. Scriabin and Messiaen both wrote music for which they saw and identified specific colours. Scriabin, more than any other composer except Messiaen, exemplifies the synaesthete. Indeed, an attempt to appreciate Scriabin's compositions without taking into consideration the synaesthesia at their source is doomed to failure. Composing actually depended upon his synaesthetic vision. It is primarily because of his capacity to use synaesthesia creatively that Scriabin made his profound contribution to modernism. It is fascinating to read Scriabin's description of his colour-sound associations: F minor was blue, "the colour of reason," D major a sunny golden, and F major "the blood red of hell" [Berman, 1999].

The link between synaesthesia and the arts has attracted controversy for over a century, spurred by the production of auditory, literary and visual art by famous individuals who report experiences synonymous with the neurological condition. Interdisciplinary debates have concerned whether synaesthesia can actively contribute to an artist's ability, whether it is a driving force or a mere idiosyncratic quirk and whether, fundamentally, it is a distinct idiopathic condition or an unusual metaphorical description of normal perception. Recent psychological and neuroscientific evidence offers a new level to the debate. Coherent patterns of a neural basis of synaesthesia have been confirmed with high spatial resolution brain imaging techniques and the link with the arts is transpiring to be more than superficial or coincidental. Moreover, the neural distinction of the synaesthete's brain may prove to be a window into a neural basis of creative cognition, and therefore conducive to the expression of creativity in various media [Mulvenna, 2007].

The real question then is, did Scriabin involuntarily see colours when he heard musical pitches or did he intentfully relate certain pitches to certain colours?

Alternative hypothesis: refutations

Doubts have been cast over the years regarding Scriabin's associations of tones and colours. Harrison [2001] commented: "In fact, there is considerable doubt about the legitimacy of the claims made on Scriabin's behalf." Galeyev and Vanechkina [56] concluded that "the nature of Scriabin's colour-tonal analogies was associative, i.e. psychological; accordingly, the existing belief that Scriabin was a distinctive, unique *synaesthete* who really saw the sounds of music, i.e. literally had an ability for co-sensations, is placed in doubt." Oliver Sacks took the stance that Scriabin's tone-colour associations "may have represented a conscious symbolism rather than actual synaesthesia" [Sacks, 2008]. Regarding visual art, de Schloezer [1987] writes that contemporary paintings, with their emphasis on purely pictorial representation without spiritual overtones, left Scriabin indifferent.

Occasionally, authors such as the Austrian visual artist Johannes Deutsch [2012] differentiate between synaesthesia as a neurological condition, in the way it is studied by medicine, psychology and neuroscience, and characterised by exceptional sensory perception, and a long-standing tradition of "synaesthetic oeuvres" in the history and theory of art and culture; the question thus emerges whether Scriabin was a "genuine" synaesthete or whether he linked musical tones to colours in *Prometheus* to generate a "synaesthetic symphony" [Deutsch, 2012].

Galeyev and Vanechkina [2001] have rather emphatically argued that Scriabin's "hearing of colours" had to do more with a musician's sensitive imagination and good ear in a non-literal, metaphorical sense, rather than synaesthesia in the neuroscientific sense. They based their reasoning on three lines of evidence: the composer's own statements as documented by his contemporaries, especially Sabaneiev; handwritten notes in the Scriabin Museum Archives; and material on his "colour hearing" published during his life-time by others. Everything that followed over a century now contains secondary or tertiary reiterations, often confounded with misapprehension. These researchers pinpoint to Sabaneiev's fundamental use of the term "association" to denote the relationship between colour and sound in his discussions in every musician's own semantics of tonalities. A plausible explanation is that Scriabin arranged associations to further his original aim of a theosophical-symbolist synthesis in his search for esoteric, universal analogies. Thus, he distinguished "spiritual" tonalities, such as F-sharp major, from "material" tonalities, such as C major and F major. In the Scriabin Museum Archives there are original manuscripts indicating different versions of note-colour combinations, supporting the premise of a system of theoretical constructs and consciously-contrived associations. Scriabin occasionally even anticipated the change of colours before tones, and further evoked "achromatic" hues beyond the visual spectrum, such as "ultra-red" or "ultra-violet."

Galeyev and Vanechkina [2001] conclude that Rimsky-Korsakov and Kandinsky might not have been synaesthetes in the clinical sense as well; instead, they might be expressing a normal ability of metaphorical thinking in their art. On the contrary, a clearcut case of synaesthesia in a musician is the example of bell ringer Konstantin K. Saradzhev (1900–1942), son of the Armenian conductor Konstantin S. Saradzhian (1877–1954), who "saw" the colours of musically-organised sounds, resembling in certain ways the synaesthete Solomon V. Sherishevsky (1886–1958), the famous "mnemonist" of Alexander Luria [1968].

The case for Scriabin's conception of a multimodal aesthetics as opposed to 'suffering' from synaesthesia as an actual neurological condition also receives support from the interview of the composer to Myers [Myers, 1914]. In true synaesthetes, on the other hand, a specific tone will always induce a particular colour, involuntarily and persistently. It is plausible that the refinement of Scriabin by his intellect and skill led him to see and develop such connections. Undoubting the inseparableness of music and philosophy, Scriabin endeavoured an integrative aesthetics: he conceived of the *Mysterium* as the synthesis of all arts, engaging all sensory modalities, in order to reach an ecstatic state and eventually a cataclysm, with the Himalayas in the background [Starcevic, 2012].

Whereas some colour-music compositions stem from true synaesthetic experience, others are wholly made up, in which case they constitute deliberate contrivances. These latter include *Prometheus* and *Mysterium* by Scriabin, *Der gelbe Klang* by Kandinsky and De Hartmann, and the *Colour Symphony* of Sir Arthur Bliss. Thought coloured music is not without intrinsic interest, the notion that colour and music can be translated into each other rests on the fallacy that a universal translation algorithm among sensory modes exists. Moreover, mixed media is not a modern invention. Odorama, smellavision, son et lumière, and laser light shows all have their historical place [Cytowic, 2002]. There are modern attempts to mathematically correlate the association between pitch and colour in Scriabin

[Lucy, 1987].

The idea of a painting and music analogy "or synaesthesia of the arts" and the demand for their synthesis was exemplified by Kandinsky in his 1912 *Almanac*. Already expressed in Plato's *Republic* ("Painting is controlled by the same laws as musical rhythm"), such a relationship had become topical since the preromantic movement, and by 1900, the "colour-music" idea was a general conviction of painters and musicians. Kandinsky was a pioneer in seriously bringing such a realisation into effect: having studied the Russian efforts, he solicited an article from Sabaneiev, a disciple of Modest Mussorgsky, on Scriabin's "colour symphony" *Prometheus*, which is based on the principle of corresponding sounds and colours [Lankheit, 1974].

Kandinsky [1974] considers the "repetition" of one method of one art, e.g. music, by means of an identical method of another art, e.g. painting, as *one* case and *one* possibility, whereby an especially powerful effect is obtained as the specific "sound" of one art reinforces and strengthens an identical "sound" in another art. Expressly for Scriabin, Kandinsky deems the composer's synthesis of music and colour a "possibility used as an inner method."

Yamawaki and Shiizuka [2006] propose that synaesthetic experience may exist at a subconscious level as a general ability of all humans and that the descriptions on coloured hearing given by Messiaen and Scriabin on their experiences might even contradict the neurological postulation of their "synaesthesia." Instead, the association of music and colours in such a context could be attributed to influences of common recognition. In the case of *Prometheus*, for example, the "coloured hearing" is not a true reflection of the composer's personal sense, but rather the common comprehension and sensibility of the musician.

Newer research suggests that the matching of colour with the 'mystic chord' in *Prometheus* is not based on an actual synaesthetic experience by Scriabin, but rather, it originates as a "compositional device" for the purpose of opening up the possibility for a 'syn-aesthetical' experience by performers and audience [Secor, 2013]. Specifically, the pre-planned use of light by means of the *Tastiera per luce* (colour photo shown on rear cover) is indispensable and complementary to the sound, in a dual acoustical and optical mode forming *one* art form, in order that the listeners would discern the higher-level harmonic content of the music and comprehend the Symbolist narrative of the drama that Scriabin intended his symphonic poem to embody [Gawboy, 2010].

Perhaps some of the perplexity of the problem can be solved if one considers the common Greek etymology of the terms *aisthēsis* (sense and sensation as in physiological psychology) and *aisthētikē* (aesthetics as in philosophy) from the verb *aisthanesthai* (to feel).

Scriabin developed a great sensitivity to the multicoloured visual impressions that often contain a musical reality at a young age. A striking example of a tone painting is found in the *Tenth Sonata*, op. 70 (1913) for piano, in which a plenitude of colours dominates, of living colours reflected in their own light, from the most sombre to the dazzlingly brilliant [Shukow, 1999].

Some of the hues Scriabin indicated for tones in *Prometheus* become evident in Scriabin's colourful fantasy when he described with exuberance his first encounter with the sea: "The sun was at first crimson, then pink, and finally a silvery brilliance flooded over the water's surface; the green of the sea water blended with the blue of the reflected sky, and the sun scattered its golden rays over the rising wave crests. It was a play of colours and shadows, a celebration of light" [Shukow, 1999]. In this case, we have an invocation to colours without tonal stimuli.

A sensible 'anthopological' explication presumes that in the distal past, mystical-religious art expressed all human secret abilities and led to ecstasy by employing all available means that affect the mind [Sabaneiev, 1974]; on a smaller scale, contemporary church service, descending from classic mystical ritual, preserves the idea of unified arts by intermingling music (chanting, bells), light (candles, chandeliers), painting (icons, mosaïcs), scent (incense, myrrh) and plastic movement (kneeling, priest acts) in one harmonious whole, to attain exaltation.

As early as the 6th century A.D., in the interior of the church of Hagia Sophia in Constantinople, marble and gold had a psychological effect on worshippers: the optical *marmarygma* ('shimmer'), linked to the acoustic properties of marble and its capacity to reflect sound waves, highlights the Eucharistic rite and *empsychosis* ('animation') and evinces the multisensory aesthetics of

Hagia Sophia through the fusion of the visual and the acoustic [Pentcheva, 2011].

Thus, at the dawn of history, humanity knew only one inchoate 'Omni-art,' in which the diverse elements of dance, music, painting formed a perplexed tissue of motoric, auditory and visual sensations; Scriabin thought that a memory of this ancient period of Omni-art had survived in the Classical Greek theatre, where all the "heterogeneous" components were closely inter-related [de Schloezer, 1987].

The various branches of the arts, after the epoch of their wholeness in antiquity, and remarkably after the Renaissance, became autonomous, reaching startling perfections independently of one another; we have such instances in music, literature, and painting [Sabaneiev, 1974]. At the turn of the 20th century, right after the advent of electricity, the arts of movement, the play of light, and the symphony of colours began to develop and reunite. Wagner formulated such ideas vaguely, but it was Scriabin who expressed them much more clearly: "All the arts must be united in one work whose exaltation will be followed by an authentic vision of a higher reality."

Scriabin saw Omni-art as a species of 'counterpoint' or 'polyphony' of the individual arts. In the 'contrapuntal' *Mysterium*, he included in the score, beyond the 'traditional aesthetics' of hearing and vision, the so-called inferior organic senses, i.e. touch, taste and olfaction, although these would still be governed by logical consistency. Those elements did not have to occur simultaneously, but, like in a fugue, their continuity could be disrupted and restored at will. The return to the primordial state of an integrative art would not be merely a recapitulation, but rather, an illumination, a transfiguration towards universal beauty [de Schloezer, 1987].

Moseley [2010] agrees: "Scriabin is often cited as a music-colour synaesthete, but it has been suggested that his aligning of colours with keys is related closely to the cycle of fifths (a series in which each note is the dominant of the one that precedes it, e.g. C – G – D – A – E – B – F-sharp – C-sharp – D-sharp etc.), suggesting that its basis was intellectual rather than purely sensory."

Gawboy and Townsend [2012] write: "One of the most widespread myths about *Prometheus* is that the *luce* part had something to do with Scriabin's alleged synaesthesia. Today, we think of synaesthesia as an involuntary neurological condition, but it is important to recognise that over the past century, the definition of synaesthesia has narrowed. One hundred years ago, "synaesthesia" could refer to a broad range of cross-sensory phenomena, regardless of whether such mappings arose through neurological, psychological, pathological, artistic, intellectual, spiritual or mystic means. These changing definitions have led to controversy over the nature of Scriabin's coloured hearing. While the majority of the concert-going public now assume Scriabin's synaesthesia was neurological in origin, Sabaneiev indicated that Scriabin deliberately constructed his system of tone-colour correspondence for its artistic and spiritual effects. It is perhaps most accurate to say that Scriabin *was* a synaesthete according to the way the phenomenon was framed during his own time period, but according to current definitions he was not."

And they continue: "The myth of the neurological origin of Scriabin's synaesthesia has had unfortunate consequences in both performance practice and scholarship. In performance, this myth (combined with the primitive notation for *luce* in the published score) has resulted in a tradition that presents the *luce* as a shifting play of colours, without nuance or other effects. In scholarship, this myth has contributed to a lack of curiosity regarding the full extent of Scriabin's colour-correspondence system. Just as the Parisian score revealed the *luce* part in *Prometheus* to be far more than colour alone, Scriabin's carefully worked-out scheme turns out to be far more analytically interesting than the spontaneous mappings typical of neurological synaesthetes."

Chemical Substances.— For the sake of thoroughness, a brief mention is made of chemically-induced synaesthesia, occasionally reported as a consequence of the use of psychoactive and hallucinogenic drugs, putatively affecting the central monoamine pathways; those experiences differ from the naturally occurring form of developemental synaesthesia in that they are transient, they are also accompanied by loss of reality monitoring, may manifest sensory combinations that otherwise do not occur naturally, and, finally, have an onset in adulhood or whenever the drug is used [Baron-Cohen and

Harrison, 1999].

In 1919 Schloezer discussed "a seemingly trivial but actually very significant fact" regarding the occasional claim by the young Scriabin that intoxication may be beneficial to creative activity and that wine offers a temporary freedom. Apparently, Scriabin showed remarkable tolerance for intoxicants, and never appeared intoxicated, no matter how much he drank. Later, particularly, after the composition of the first five *Sonatas*, he completely changed his attitude toward alcohol: he came to see it as a sign of spiritual decadence, and the need for artificial stimulants as an index of inferiority, immaturity and lack of mystical insight. He occasionally drank wine, especially after his concert appearances, but never abused such practice. He would even say, "I have no need of wine" [de Schloezer, 1987].

In 1925 Sabaneiev reiterated that Scriabin refused the idea of perceiving "visions" of colour in music under the influence of drugs, as anyone can become a "synaesthete" not spiritually but chemically, and resentfully declined any offer to change his consciousness by such "brute means" [Galeyev and Vanechkina, 2001].

SYNAESTHETIC
MECHANISMS

Modern vistas

THE TERM 'SYNAESTHESIA' has been used loosely to report a 'mixing of senses.' An important consideration when discussing "synaesthetic experiences" by artists is to make a distinction between involuntary, automatic sensations on one hand, and the imagery that arises from imagination on the other [Baron-Cohen and Harrison, 1999]. The practical problem is that direct evidence through modern objective tests cannot be gathered from musicians of the past in order to make an accurate diagnosis. One may clear the confusion by distinguishing beween developmental synaesthesia, acquired synaesthesia secondary to neuropathological alterations (e.g. sensory 'leakage' and colour hyperaesthesia as a result of optical lesions), synaesthesias induced by psychoactive substances, and pseudosynaesthesias that are triggered voluntarily either as a meta-phor/analogy or as a learned association. One criterion for the presence of true developmental synaesthesia is a subject's consistency in reporting e.g. colour description.

With regard to the auditory system, in the cochlea, low tones are picked up near the tip (helicotrema), high tones near the oval window, and there is a point-to-point correspondence between the cochlea and the acoustic cortical area on Heschl's gyrus on the su-pratemporal plane [Netter, 1977]: in humans and the other primates, high tones are transmitted to the frontal end of the acoustic area, and low tones to the occipital end of the acoustic area (see drawing on rear cover of the book).

Theorised neurobiological causes of synaesthesia include: (a) preserved neural connectivity, i.e. the persistence of immature pathways, connecting visual and auditory cortical regions, in adulthood, owing to a failure in the epigenetic pruning of the developmental surplass; (b) a disconnection of visual and optical pathways and a 'bypass' activation of limbic-cortical circuits, particularly involving the posterior inferotemporal cortex and the parieto-occipital junction, which both participate in colour perception; (c) a genetic component coding for inherited traits (migration and maturation mechanisms, and apoptosis) that preserve aberrant neural connections; (d) a breakdown in cognitive modules with the consequence of sounds e.g. having visual attributes; (e) cross-modal matching, similar to what may occur in non-synaesthetic subjects [Baron-Cohen and Harrison, 1999].

Synaesthesia may be an "umbrella term" that encompasses distinct groups with independent probabilities of expression, including labelled coloured sequence synaesthesias, coloured music synaesthesias, non-visual sequel synaesthesias, spatial sequence synaesthesias, and coloured sensation synaesthesias. This may point to distinct underlying mechanisms and different genetic bases [Novich et al., 2011].

The 'cross-modal matching theory' is based on the findings that normal adult subjects exhibit a noticeable consistency in rating auditory-visual "synaesthetic metaphors" with regard to loudness, pitch, and brightness: loudness and pitch express themselves metaphorically as greater brightness, and brightness expresses itself as greater loudness and higher pitch. Since people, in evaluating synaesthetic metaphors, emulate the characteristics of synaesthetic perception, Marks [1982] suggested that synaesthesia in perception and synaesthesia in language may both emanate from the same source, i.e., a phenomenological similarity in the makeup of the sensory experiences of different modalities.

Synaesthetes who report colour sensations in response to music and other sounds tend to choose preciser colours with higher consistency when given a set of sounds of varying pitch, timbre and composition (single notes or dyads), compared to controls. Nonetheless, both controls and synaesthetes appear to use similar heuristics for matching between auditory and visual domains (such as pitch to lightness), indicating that, in synaesthesia, some of the normal mechanisms of cross-modal perception might be recruited, as opposed to distinct or "privileged" pathways between unimodal auditory and unimodal visual areas which would not be found in non-synaesthetic adults [Ward et al., 2006a].

On the other hand, by investigating the white matter

correlates of coloured-music synaesthesia and patterns of connectivity between visual and auditory association areas, using diffusion tensor imaging (DTI) to trace white matter tracts in temporal and occipital lobe regions in synaesthetes and matched non-synaesthetic controls, synaesthetes possess hemispheric patterns of fractional anisotropy, an index of white matter integrity, in the inferior fronto-occipital fasciculus, a major pathway that connects visual and auditory association areas to frontal cortical areas. White matter integrity in the right inferior fronto-occipital fasciculus is significantly greater in synaesthetes than in controls, and correlates with scores on audiovisual tests of the Synaesthesia Battery, especially in white matter underlying the right fusiform gyrus, suggesting that enhanced white matter connectivity is involved in enhanced cross-modal associations [Zamm et al., 2013].

Historically, the first convincing account of synaesthesia in the literature, which influenced some of the early theories, was published in 1812 by Georg Sachs, in Latin; that dissertation concerned the albinism of himself and of his sister, as well as synaesthesia involving colours for music and simple sequences, such as numbers, days and letters [Jewanski et al., 2009]. In 1864, Chabalier [1864] introduced the term 'pseudochromaesthesia' in discussing the similarities and the differences among synaesthesia, illusions, and hallucinations; he made the distinction of synaesthesia as a form of an illusion, rather than a hallucination, based on the argument that illusions require an object to be elicited, whereas hallucinations do not [Jewanski et al., 2011]. An early book on colour theory, including an attempt at exploring the interdependence of colours and music, was presented in the late 19th century by Jugenstil artist Joseph Sattler (1867–1931). He used examples of musical scores by Schumann, Franck and Wagner, which he marked with colour scales, and provided equations such as "grey + green = serious *(ernst)*" and "blue + red = joyous *(freudich)*" [Sattler, 1896].

In auditory-visual synaesthesia, sounds automatically elicit conscious and reliable visual experiences. It is unknown whether adult audiovisual synaesthesia resembles auditory-induced visual illusions that sometimes occur in the general population or whether it resembles the electrophysiological deflection over occipital sites which is noted in infancy and resembles synaesthesia. There are differences between synaesthetes and controls that emerge early (100 msec after a tone onset), tending to lie in deflections of the auditory-evoked potential (e.g., auditory N1, P2, and N2) rather than the presence of an additional posterior deflection. Differences occur irrespective of what synaesthetes attend to (although attention has a late effect). Thus, differences between synaesthetes and others occur early in time, and synaesthesia may differ qualitatively from similar effects found in infants or certain auditory-induced visual illusions in adults [Goller et al., 2009].

Art is created, perceived and appreciated by human brains. Therefore, authors argue that a scientific account of art, driven by research in the neurosciences, is a realistic goal. One aspect of art, termed 'visual music,' is concerned with how the visual arts can capture, and be inspired by, properties of music (e.g. its non-depicting nature), and also with how music and visual art can be directly combined. People with synaesthesia may experience complex visual photisms while listening to music. The term 'visual music' refers to works of art in which both hearing and vision are directly or indirectly stimulated. Our ability to create, perceive, and appreciate visual music is hypothesised to rely on the same multisensory processes that support auditory-visual (AV) integration in other contexts. Studies of synaesthesia in which sound evokes vision and studies of cross-modal biases in non-synaesthetes reveal non-arbitrary mappings between visual and auditory properties (e.g. high-pitch sounds being smaller and brighter). Synaesthetic AV animations are generally preferred over control conditions by non-synaesthetes. Thus, non-arbitrary AV mappings, present in the experiences of synaesthetes, can be readily appreciated by members of the general population and may underpin our tendency to engage with certain forms of art. The experiences of people with auditory-visual synaesthesia can be used to reveal the structure of auditory-visual mappings that exist in the wider population; such mappings may play a role in our ability to appreciate 'visual music' as an art form. The experiences of people who have this form of synaesthesia may provide a rich source of motivation to participate in both visual art and music. The study of synaesthesia and multisensory integration offers the potential to widen the exploration of a holistic approach to the scientific understanding of art

[Ward et al., 2008a].

Synaesthetes may show heightened creativity as a result of being able to form meaningful associations between disparate stimuli (e.g. colour and sound). Synaesthetes tend to be more engaged in creative arts, depending on the type of synaesthesia; e.g., synaesthetes experiencing vision from music are far more likely to play an instrument than other synaesthetic counterparts. Such a tendency is likely to have a different mechanism to psychometric measures of creativity, plausibly with no direct link between the two [Ward et al., 2008b].

Concerning pitch-colour correspondence, synaesthetes may be able to place their colour responses even to notes falling between adjacent semitones (quartertones), compared to controls [de Thornley Head, 2006]. In some cases, synaesthetes may experience colours in response to written musical notation, graphemes and heard music; in those cases, the synaesthetically experienced colour may influence the reading and playing of music as a sensory-motor transformation, but not verbal colour naming [Ward et al., 2006b]. Of the different types of synaesthesia, most have colour as the concurrent perception, with concurrent perceptions of smell or taste being rare. A case was described of a female musician who experiences different tastes in response to hearing different musical tone intervals, and who makes use of usch synaesthetic sensations in the complex task of identifying tone intervals [Beeli et al., 2005].

NEUROAESTHETICS

THE EXPERIMENTS OF NEUROAESTHETICS focus on the properties of and the interactions between a triad of neural systems that emerge from aesthetic experiences: sensory-motor, emotion-valuation, and meaning-knowledge circuitries [Chatterjee and Vartanian, 2014].

The study of performing arts such as dance, in addition to music and painting, in the framework of Neuroaesthetics, i.e. the field that attempts to decipher the neural processes that underlie aesthetic experience, suggests a possible role of visual and sensorimotor brain areas in an automatic aesthetic response to dance, and particularly a system comprising 'mirror neuron areas' in the premotor and parietal cortices for perceiving and executing actions; the brain network for implicit aesthetic perception of dance further includes the superior temporal sulcus and the occipital cortex

[Calvo-Merino et al., 2008].

Figure 7 Portrait of Alexander Scriabin (1872–1915) sketched by the author. Black pastel on paper, 295 × 226 mm, 16 February 1987. Based on the composer's favourite photo, taken in 1908 in Berlin by Hans Dursthoff [Camner, 1981].

York [2010] argues that, if painters are neurologists, as Semir Zeki has suggested, with a province in the visual brain, then musicians are neurologists who manipulate the auditory brain of audiences for their aesthetic pleasure. Zeki [2002] actually suggested that

Richard Wagner created his 'Tristan chord' being knowledgeable about the operations of the mind and relying on ancient laws of tonality that derive from the nature of our perceptive mechanisms, without though having any direct knowledge about brain tissue; through a profound understanding of the workings of the musical brain, Wagner delved into it with techniques that are unique to artists. In that sense, "Wagner was a neurobiologist." Would it not then be appropriate to also consider Scriabin a neuroscientist, delving with his 'Mystic chord' into the integrative action of the human nervous system?

Scriabin sought his formative spirituality in a fantastic synthesis of the arts, interlaced with colours, poetic elements, perfumes, voluptuous flower scents, even tactile association (caresses) between audience and performers. "The creator, exerting his influence on the listeners, supposing the action is musical in nature, is reciprocally influenced by them" [de Schloezer, 1987].

A neurobiological topic that may be relevant to bring up is the theme of mirror neurons. Mirror neurons of musicians combine auditory and visual (action observation) systems and may instigate a bidirectional inter-

action between players and audiences. Performers feel
the emotional essence of the music and communicate it
to the listeners; an audience does not merely observe or
hear a performer, but perceives emotional content
[Molnar-Szakacs and Overy, 2006; Svard, 2010]. The
reciprocal may also be happening: the affective state of
audience members, individual or collective, may mirror
it on an actor, a soloist, a conductor, or an orchestra.
Musicians have known all along that each performance
of the same piece is different and unique.

Besides cross-activation of two sensory areas, the synaesthetic experience may be modulated by attention
and also require additional binding processes, which
involve the inferior parietal lobe. Such an involvement
could reflect a 'hyperbinding process' which combines
real and synaesthetic sensory experiences into a common percept. Thus, the original formulation of the
cross-activation theory has been extended to a two-
stage model, which includes the binding process
through parietal cortical areas [Speecht, 2012]. In particular, based on fMRI studies during non-linguistic
sound perception (chords and pure tones), the key
brain region involved in auditory-visual synaesthesia

appears to be the left inferior parietal cortex, an area known to be involved in multimodal integration, feature-binding, and attention-guidance, whereas area V4, which is related to colour vision and form-processing, does not seem to differ in activation between diagnosed synaesthetes and non-synaesthetic controls. Therefore, the parietal cortex may act as a sensory nexus in auditory-visual synaesthesia, and even as a common neural correlate for other forms of synaesthesia [Neufeld et al., 2012].

On occasion, neurology may provide insight into artistic creativity. A patient after a small left paramedian thalamic infarct reported some unusual features. He became "more sensitive to the hidden beauty of nature" and "wanted to live and paint spontaneously, explore the world, and represent it in its raw strength," having lost interest in impressionism. It was the use of the left hand that led him into this new artistic dimension: "...he discovered that figures executed with his left hand had more emotional strength and bolder colours, whereas, in those painted with the right hand, the lines, contours, and perspectives were clearer. He realised that his creativity was increased by the use of the left hand." The same subject painted with the left, right, or both hands, demonstrating "that the painting produced using the left hand employed more vivid colours" [Schott, 2012].

A different patient suffering from dementia and primary progressive aphasia associated with documented corticobasal degeneration, the brunt of the illness was borne by the left frontoinsular, temporal and striatal regions; she used a complex but exact scheme to very precisely represent Ravel's *Boléro* pictorially, the musical components featured in every bar being translated into visual components in a gouache painting she entitled *Unravelling Boléro*, showing de novo transmodal creativity which comprised auditory-to-visual transformation, six years before her symptoms began [Seeley et al., 2008].

Envoy

Synaesthesia provides a window into the neural correlates of cross-modal associations. Can the mind of musicians open up windows to probe into brain function in general? Can the arts and the humanities substantially contribute to the study of the human brain? There is a common characteristic, independent of learning or culture, to all that is experienced as 'beautiful,' which is common to all and peculiar to no one; that characteristic lies in a simple neurobiological fact, that whenever an individual experiences beauty, regardless of whether the source is visual, musical, moral or mathematical, there is a correlate in the form of metabolic activity in an anatomical component of the emotional brain, namely field A1 of the medial orbitofrontal cortex [Zeki, 2014]. The medial orbitofrontal cortex and the adjacent cingulate cortex respond to various sources of pleasure, including music [Ishizu and Zeki, 2011] and even architectural space [Vartanian et al., 2013].

Artists are driven by an urge for impact. Science can look at their work to find a "naïve physics" that uncovers deep and ancient insights into the workings of the mind; the discrepancies between the real world and the world depicted by artists may reveal as much about the brain within us as the artist reveals about the world around us [Cavanagh, 2005].

In 1919 Boris de Schloezer [1987], in his account of the life of Alexander Nikolaevich (figure 7), noted: "To

Scriabin the ultimate reality was Omni-art, of which music is only a component part." In 2002, cell biologist Christian de Duve, the discoverer of the lysosome and the peroxisome, would conclude his own account of the saga of life on a concordant note: "Much has changed since the day when I first became aware of the mysteries of the Universe. I have experienced the almost voluptuous thrill of understanding, the rare flash of illumination…And I have also vibrated in different registers, in resonance with the poets, writers, artists, and musicians who have moved me by their works and performances. On exceptional occasions, I have felt close to something ineffable, utterly mysterious but real, at least to me, an entity that, for want of a better term, I call Ultimate Reality" [de Duve, 2002].

BIBLIOGRAPHY

Altenmüller, E., "Alexander Scriabin: his chronic right-hand pain and its impact on his piano compositions", in *Music, Neurology, and Neuroscience: Historical Connections and Perspectives—Progress in Brain Research*, E. Altenmüller, S. Finger, and F. Boller, Eds., vol. 216, pp. 197–215, Elsevier, Amsterdam, Holland – Oxford, UK – Waltham, MA, USA, 2015.

Altschuler, M., "The young Scriabin I remember," *Clavier Magazine (Evanston)*, vol. 11, no. 1, pp. 31–32, 1972.

Antcliffe, H., "The Significance of Scriabin," *Musical Quarterly (Oxford)*, vol. 10, no. 3, pp. 333–345, 1924.

Ballard, L. M., "Alexander Scriabin's centenary revival in Soviet era Russia," *Journal of the Scriabin Society of America*, vol. 14, no. 1, pp. 40–49, 2010.

Baron-Cohen, S. and J. Harrison, "Synesthesia: a challenge for Developmental Cognitive Neuroscience," in *Neurodevelopmental Disorders*, H. Tager-Flusberg, Ed., pp. 491–503, MIT Press, Cambridge, MA, USA, 1999.

Bartlett, F. C., "Charles Samuel Myers, 1873–1946," *Obituary*

Notices of Fellows of the Royal Society (London), vol. 5, no. 16, pp. 767–777, 1948.

Baylor, M., *Scriabin—Selected Works for the Piano*, Alfred Publishing, Van Nuys, CA, USA, 1974.

Beeli, G., M. Esslen, and L. Jäncke, "Synaesthesia: when coloured sounds taste sweet," *Nature*, vol. 434, no. 7029, p. 38, 2005.

Belsa, I. F., *Alexander Nikolajewitsch Skrjabin* (Übersetzung von C. Hellmundt), Verlag Neue Musik, Berlin, DDR, 1986.

Berman, G., "Synesthesia and the arts," *Leonardo*, vol. 32, no. 1, pp. 15–22, 1999.

Boake, C., "Édouard Claparède and the auditory verbal learning test," *Journal of Clinical and Experimental Neuropsychology*, vol. 22, no. 2, pp. 286–292, 2000.

Bowers, F., *Scriabin—A Biography of the Russian Composer*, Kodansha International, Tokyo, Japan – Palo Alto, CA, USA, 1969, p. 204.

Bowers, F., "Centennial reflections: A Scriabin centennial feature," *Clavier Magazine (Evanston)*, vol. 11, no. 1, pp. 17–20, 1972.

Brust, J. C. M., "Music and the neurologist: a historical perspective," *Annals of the New York Academy of Sciences*, vol. 930, pp. 143–152, 2001.

Brust, J. C. M., "Music and the neurologist: a historical perspective," in *The Cognitive Neuroscience of Music*, I. Peretz and R. Zatorre, Eds., pp. 181–191, Oxford University Press, Oxford, UK, 2003.

Butler, R. K., *The Influence of Theosophy on the Tradition of Speculative and Esoteric Theories of Music* (Ph.D. Thesis), Queensland Conservatorium, Griffith University, Brisbane, Australia, 2013.

Calvo-Merino, B., C. Jola, D. E. Glaser, and P. Haggard, "Towards a sensorimotor aesthetics of performing art," *Consciousness and Cognition*, vol. 17, no. 3, pp. 911–922, 2008.

Camner, J., *Great Composers in Historic Photographs—From the 1860s to the 1960s*, Dover Publications, New York, NY, USA, 1981, p. 98.

Cavanagh, P., "The artist as neuroscientist," *Nature*, vol. 434, no. 7031, pp. 301–307, 2005.

Chabalier, G., "De la pseudochromesthésie," *Journal de Médecine de Lyon*, vol. 1, no. 2, pp. 92–102, 1864.

Chatterjee, A. and O. Vartanian, "Neuroaesthetics," *Trends in Cognitive Sciences*, vol. 18, no. 7, pp. 370–375, 2014.

Claparède, É., "Sur l'audition colorée," *Revue Philosophique de la France et de l'Étranger (Paris)*, vol. 49, no. 5, pp. 515–517, 1900.

Claparède, É., "Persistance de l'audition colorée," *Comptes*

Rendus Hebdomadaires des Séances et Mémoires de la Société de Biologie (Paris), vol. 55, no. X/31, pp. 1257–1259, 1903.

Claparède, É., *Rapports et Comptes Rendus du Congrès International de Philosophie—IIème Session*, Henry Kündig, Geneva, Switzerland, 1905, pp. 1–974.

Clément, J.-Y., *Alexandre Scriabine ou l'Ivresse des sphères*, Actes Sud/Classica, Arles, France, 2015.

Cohn, A., *Hilde Somer plays Scriabin*, Mercury Record Productions/Conelco Corporation, Chicago, IL, USA, 1968.

Cytowic, R. E., *Synesthesia: A Union of the Senses*, Springer-Verlag, New York, NY, USA, 1989.

Cytowic, R. E., *Synesthesia: A Union of the Senses*, 2nd edn., MIT Press, Cambridge, MA, USA, 2002, p. 319.

de Duve, C., *Life Evolving: Molecules, Mind, and Meaning*, Oxford University Press, Oxford – New York, 2002.

de Schloezer, B., *Scriabin—Artist and Mystic* (translated by N. Slonimsky), University of California Press, Berkeley, CA, USA, 1987.

de Thornley Head, P., "Synaesthesia: pitch-colour isomorphism in RGB-space?", *Cortex*, vol. 42, no. 2, pp. 164–174, 2006.

Delson, V., *Scriabin*, Izdatelstvo «Muzika»/Melodiya, Moscow, USSR, 1971.

Deutsch, J., "Synaesthesia and synergy in art: Gustav Mahler's Symphony no. 2 in C minor as an example of interactive music visualization," in *Sensory Perception—Mind and Matter*, F. G. Barth, P. Giampieri-Deutsch, and H.-D. Klein, Eds., pp. 215–235, Springer-Verlag, Vienna, Austria, 2012.

Drozdov, I., M. Kidd, and I. M. Modlin, "Evolution of one-handed piano compositions," *Journal of Hand Surgery*, vol. 33, no. 5, pp. 780–786, 2008.

Duguay, M., *Jean Michel Jarre, le Magicien du Son et de la Lumière*, 2*ème* édn., Coëtquen Éditions, Janzé, France, 2011.

Eaglefield Hull, A., "A survey of the pianoforte works of Scriabin," *Musical Quarterly (Oxford)*, vol. 2, no. 4, pp. 601–614, 1916a.

Eaglefield Hull, A., *Scriabin: A Great Russian Tone-Poet*, Kegan Paul, Trench, Trubner & Co., Ltd., London, UK, 1916b.

Edel, T., *Piano Music for One Hand*, Indiana University Press, Bloomington, IN, USA, 1994.

Eustache, F., B. Desgranges, and P. Messerli, "Édouard Claparède et la mémoire humaine," *Revue Neurologique (Paris)*, vol. 152, no. 10, pp. 602–610, 1996.

Franke, K., *Der Pianist Scriabin (Eine Einführung)*, Ariola Eurodisc, Gütersloh, West Germany, 1973.

Galeyev, B. M. and I. L. Vanechkina, "Was Scriabin a synesthete?", *Leonardo*, vol. 34, no. 4, pp. 357–361, 2001.

Garcia, E. E., "Rachmaninoff and Scriabin: creativity and suffering in talent and genius," *Psychoanalytic Review*, vol. 91, no. 3, pp. 423-442, 2004.

Garvelmann, D., *An Essay on Scriabin's 24 Preludes, Op. 11*, Vox-Turnabout/Moss Music Group, New York, NY, USA, 1982.

Gawboy, A., *Alexander Scriabin's Theurgy in Blue—Esotericism and the Analysis of 'Prometheus: Poem of Fire' op. 60* (Ph.D. Thesis). Yale University School of Music, New Haven, CT, USA, 2010.

Gawboy, A. M. and J. Townsend, "Scriabin and the possible," *MTO—Journal of the Society for Music Theory*, vol. 18, no. 2, pp. 1–21, 2012.

Goller, A. I., L. J. Otten, and J. Ward, "Seeing sounds and hearing colors: an event-related potential study of auditory-visual synesthesia," *Journal of Cognitive Neuroscience*, vol. 21, no. 10, pp. 1869–1881, 2009.

Gorenstein, F., *Scriabine: roman* (traduit par A. Coldefy-Faucard), Éditions Calmann-Lévy, Paris, France, 1992.

Gunst, Y., *A. N. Scriabin i ego tvorestvo* [A. N. Scriabin and His Work], Rossiyskoye Muzykalnoye Izdatelstvo – Éditions Russes de Musique, Moscow, 1915.

Harrison, J., *Synaesthesia: The Strangest Thing*, Oxford University Press, Oxford, UK, 2001.

Hope, A., "Revival of a musical mystic," *Life Magazine (Chicago)*, vol. 69, no. 16, pp. 72–76, 1970.

Ione, A., "Neurology, synaesthesia, and painting," *International Review of Neurobiology*, vol. 74, pp. 69–78, 2006.

Ione, A. and C. Tyler, "Neuroscience, history and the arts—Synesthesia: is F-sharp colored violet?", Journal of the History of the Neurosciences, vol. 13, no. 1, pp. 58–65, 2004.

Ishizu, T. and S. Zeki, "Toward a brain-based theory of beauty," *PLoS ONE*, vol. 6, no. 7, pp. 1–10, 2011. doi: 10.1371/journal.pone.0021852.

Jewanski, J., S. A. Day, and J. Ward, "A colorful albino—the first documented case of synaesthesia by Georg Tobias Ludwig Sachs in 1812," *Journal of the History of the Neurosciences*, vol. 18, no. 3, pp. 293–303, 2009.

Jewanski, J., J. Simner, S. A. Day, and J. Ward, "The development of a scientific understanding of synesthesia from early case studies (1849–1873)," *Journal of the History of the Neurosciences*, vol. 20, no. 4, pp. 284–305, 2011.

Kandinsky, W., "On stage composition," in *The Blaue Reiter Almanac Edited by Wassily Kandinsky and Franz Marc: New Documentary Edition* (translated by H. Falkenstein, M. Terzian, and G. Hinderlie), K. Lankheit, Ed., pp. 190–206, Viking Press, New York, NY, USA, 1974.

Kay, C. and C. Mulvenna, "Synaesthesia, neurology and language," in *Progress in Colour Studies: Volume II. Psychological*

Myers, C. S., *An Introduction to Experimental Psychology*, Cambridge University Press, Cambridge, UK – G. P. Putnam's Sons, New York, NY, USA, 1911b.

Myers, C. S., "Two cases of synaesthesia", *British Journal of Psychology*, vol. 7, no. 1, pp. 112–117, 1914.

Netter, F. H., *The CIBA Collection of Medical Illustrations, Vol. I: Nervous System*, CIBA, Summit, NJ, USA, 1977, pp. 64–65.

Neufeld, J., C. Sinke, W. Dillo, H. M. Emrich, G. R. Szycik, D. Dima, S. Bleich, and M. Zedler, "The neural correlates of coloured music: a functional MRI investigation of auditory-visual synaesthesia," *Neuropsychologia*, vol. 50, no. 1, pp. 85–89, 2012.

Novich, S., S. Cheng, and D. M. Eagleman, "Is synaesthesia one condition or many? A large-scale analysis reveals subgroups," *Journal of Neuropsychology*, vol. 5, no. 2, pp. 353–371, 2011.

Peacock, K., "Synesthetic perception: Alexander Scriabin's color hearing," *Music Perception*, vo. 2, no. 4, pp. 483–506, 1985.

Pearce, J. M. S., "Synaesthesia," *European Neurology*, vol. 57, no. 2, pp. 120–124, 2007.

Pentcheva, B. V., "Hagia Sophia and multisensory aesthetics," *Gesta—International Center of Medieval Art*, vol. 50, no. 2, pp. 93–111, 2011.

Pollack, B., "Erinnerungen an Moritz Moszkowski," *Berliner Tageblatt und Handels-Zeitung*, vol. 54, pp. 2–3, 14 March 1925.

Pollak, T. A., C. M. Mulvenna, and M. F. Lythgoe, "De novo artistic behaviour following brain injury," *Frontiers in Neurology and Neuroscience (Basel)*, vol. 22, pp. 75–88, 2007.

Powell, J., "Skryabin, Aleksandr Nikolaevich," in *The New Grove Dictionary of Music and Musicians*, 2nd edn., S. Sadie and J. Tyrell, Eds., vol. 23, pp. 485–495, Macmillan, London, UK, 2000.

Rimington, A. W., *Colour-Music: The Art of Mobile Colour*, Hutchinson & Co., London, UK – Frederick A. Stokes Co., New York, NY, USA, 1912.

Rist, X., *Scriabine: Les Trois Cahiers d'Études pour Piano—Un Entretien avec Nikita Magaloff (Commentaire)*, Auvidis Valois, Paris, France, 1994, pp. 4–6.

Rodgers, J., "Four Preludes ascribed to Yulian Skriabin," *19th-Century Music*, vol. 6, no. 3, pp. 213–219, 1983.

Rudakova, Y. N. and A. I. Kandinsky, *Aleksandr Nikolaevich Scriabin*, Izdatelstvo «Muzika», Moscow, USSR, 1980.

Rudakova, Y. N. and A. I. Kandinsky, *Scriabin: His Life and Times* (translated by T. Chistyakova), Paganiana Publications, Neptune City, NJ, USA, 1984.

Rüger, C., *Individuality in Scriabin's Symphonic Works* (Lines

Notes, translated by R. A. Jordan), Philips Phonographische Industrie, Amsterdam, Holland, 1980, pp. 3–6.

Runciman, J. F., "Noises, smells and colours," *Musical Quarterly (Oxford)*, vol. 1, no. 2, pp. 149–161, 1915.

Sabaneiev, L., "Scriabin's *Prometheus* [1912]," in *The Blaue Reiter Almanac Edited by Wassily Kandinsky and Franz Marc: New Documentary Edition* (translated by H. Falkenstein, M. Terzian, and G. Hinderlie), K. Lankheit, Ed., pp. 127–140, Viking Press, New York, NY, USA, 1974.

Sacks, O. W., *Musicophilia: Tales of Music and the Brain*, Picador Books, London, UK, 2008.

Sattler, J., *Meine Harmonie*, Joseph A. Stargardt Verlag, Berlin, Germany, 1896.

Schonberg, H. C., "Scriabin and Rachmaninoff: mysticism and melancholy," in *The Lives of the Great Composers*, vol. 2, pp. 197–209, Futura Publications Ltd., London, 1975.

Schott, G. D., "Pictures as a neurological tool: lessons from enhanced and emergent artistry in brain disease," *Brain (Oxford)*, vol. 135, no. 6, pp. 1947–1963, 2012.

Scriabine, A., *Notes et Réflexions* (Carnets inédits traduits du russe et présentés par Marina Scriabine), Éditions Klincksieck, Paris, France, 1979.

Scriabine, M., "Introduction," in *Scriabin—Artist and Mystic* (translated by N. Slonimsky), B. de Schloezer, pp. 1–20, University of California Press, Berkeley, CA, USA, 1987.

Secor, T. M., *Mystic Chord Harmonic and Light Transformations in Alexander Scriabin's 'Prometheus'* (M.A. Thesis), University of Oregon School of Music, Eugene, OR, USA, 2013.

Seeley, W. W., B. R. Matthews, R. K. Crawford, M. L. Gorno-Tempini, D. Foti, I. R. Mackenzie, and B. L. Miller, "Unravelling *Boléro*: progressive aphasia, transmodal creativity and the right posterior neocortex," *Brain (Oxford)*, vol. 131, no. 1, pp. 39–49, 2008.

Shaborkina, T., *Notes on Scriabin's 24 Preludes, Op. 11*, Melodiya/USSR Ministry of Culture, Moscow, USSR, 1980.

Shaborkina, T., *Notes on Scriabin's Piano Works*, Melodiya/USSR Ministry of Culture, Moscow, USSR, 1982.

Shukow, I., *Alexander Skrjabin und Seine Sonaten: Eine Betrachtung*, Telos Music, Mechernich, Germany – Tecval SA, Vallorbe, Switzerland, 1999, pp. 4–14.

Sinha, A., "Of fragrant shapes and colourful sounds: the world of a synaesthete," *Journal of Biosciences*, vol. 26, no. 2, pp. 123–124, 2001.

Skans, P., *Symphony No. 1 and Prometheus* (Cover Text, translated by A. Barnett), BIS Grammofon Aktiebolaget, Djursholm, Sweden, 1991.

Speecht, K., "Synaesthesia: cross activations, high interconnectivity, and a parietal hub," *Translational Neuroscience*, vol.

3, no. 1, pp. 15–21, 2012.

Starcevic, V., "The life and music of Alexander Scriabin: megalomania revisited," *Australasian Psychiatry*, vol. 20, no. 1, pp. 57–60, 2012.

Starr, G. G., *Feeling Beauty: The Neuroscience of Aesthetic Experience*, MIT Press, Cambridge, MA, USA, 2013, pp. 79–80.

Steinberg, H., "Electrotherapeutic disputes: the 'Frankfurt Council' of 1891," *Brain*, vol. 134, no. 4, pp. 1229–1243, 2011.

Steinberg, H. and A. Wagner, "Wilhelm Erb's years in Leipzig (1880–1883) and their impact on the history of neurology," *European Neurology*, vol. 70, no. 5–6, pp. 267–275, 2013.

Svard, L., "The musician's guide to the brain: how to use brain science in the study of music," *Music Teachers National Association e-Journal*, vol. 1, no. 3, pp. 2–11, 2010.

Triarhou, L. C., *The Berlin Ophthalmologist Bernhard Pollack: Neurohistology Scholar and Devout Musician*, Lulu Press, Raleigh, NC, USA, 2011.

Tuffs, A., *Die Heidelberger Universitäts-Hautklinik wird 100 Jahre alt*, Presse und Öffentlichkeitsarbeit des Universitätsklinikums und der Medizinischen Fakultät der Universität, Heidelberg, 2008.

Valentine, C. W., *An Introduction to the Experimental Psychology of Beauty*, T. C. & E. C. Jack, London and Edinburgh, UK – Dodge Publishing Co., New York, NY, USA, 1913.

van Campen, C., *The Hidden Sense: Synesthesia in Art and Science*, MIT Press, Cambridge, MA, USA, 2008, pp. 50–53.

van den Hoogen, E., *Alexander Nikolajewitsch Scriabin* (translated by C. R. Williams), Pathé Marconi/EMI Electrola GmbH, Cologne, West Germany, 1979.

Vartanian, O., G. Navarrete, A. Chatterjee, L. B. Fich, H. Leder, C. Modroño, M. Nadal, N. Rostrup, and M. Skov, "Impact of contour on aesthetic judgments and approach-avoidance decisions in architecture," Proceedings of the National Academy of Sciences of USA, vol. 110, suppl. 2, pp. 10446–10453, 2013.

Ward, J., B. Huckstep, and E. Tsakanikos, "Sound-colour synaesthesia: to what extent does it use cross-modal mechanisms common to us all?", *Cortex*, vol. 42, no. 2, pp. 264–280, 2006a.

Ward, J., E. Tsakanikos, and A. Bray, "Synaesthesia for reading and playing musical notes," *Neurocase*, vol. 12, no. 1, pp. 27–34, 2006b.

Ward, J., S. Moore, D. Thompson-Lake, S. Salih, and B. Beck, "The aesthetic appeal of auditory-visual synaesthetic perceptions in people without synesthesia," *Perception*, vol. 37, no. 8, pp. 1285–1296, 2008a.

Ward, J., D. Thompson-Lake, R. Ely, and F. Kaminski, "Synaesthesia, creativity and art: what is the link?" *British Journal of Psychology*, vol. 99, no. 1, pp. 127–141, 2008b.

Warren, J. D., "Variations on the musical brain," *Journal of the Royal Society of Medicine (London)*, vol. 92, no. 11, pp. 571–575, 1999.

Witztum E. and V. Lerner, "Alexander Nikolaevich Scriabin (1872–1915): enlightenment or illness?", *Journal of Medical Biography*, vol. 23, 2015 (online first, 6 June 2014, doi: 10.1177/0967772014537151).

Yamawaki, K. and H. Shiizuka, "Synesthesia and common recognition concerning music and colour," *Proceedings of the Institution of Mechanical Engineers, Part I: Journal of Systems and Control Engineering*, vol. 220, no. 8, pp. 735–743, 2006.

York III, G. K., "The neurologist in the concert hall and the musician at the bedside," in *Neurology of Music*, F. Clifford Rose, Ed., pp. 61–72, Imperial College Press, London, UK, 2010.

Zamm, A., G. Schlaug, D. M. Eagleman, and P. Loui, "Pathways to seeing music: enhanced structural connectivity in colored-music synesthesia," *Neuroimage*, vol. 74, no. 1, pp. 359–366, 2013.

Zeki, S., "Neural concept formation and art: Dante, Michelangelo, Wagner," *Journal of Consciousness Studies*, vol. 9, no. 3, pp. 53–76, 2002.

Zeki, S., "Neurobiology and the Humanities," *Neuron*, vol. 84, no. 1, pp. 12–14, 2014.

SUMMARY

The book delves into the coupling of tones and colours in the music of the avant-garde Russian composer and pianist, Alexander N. Scriabin (1872–1915). Scriabin is often mentioned in the scientific and art literature as a synaesthete, in tandem with other composers and painters. However, in reviewing his older biographies and direct testimonies, the question surfaces — notwithstanding experimental neurological confirmation — whether, rather than 'suffering' from synaesthesia as a medical condition, Scriabin willfully indited auditory, visual, olfactory and tactile elements into his late composing act, aiming at a multisensory aesthetics, i.e. a union of all senses in both performers and audiences. A special reference is made to Scriabin's attendance of the 1904 International Congress of Philosophy, organised by the neurologist Édouard Claparède (1873–1940) in Geneva, and to the 1914 encounter with the physician and psychologist Charles S. Myers (1873–1946) at the University of Cambridge. Inborn synaesthesia is disentangled from the consciously contrived, multisensory aesthetics. In Scriabin's case, the word 'synaesthesia' might more accurately pertain to philosophical aesthetics *(aisthētikē)* than psychophysiological sensation *(aisthēsis)*. Scriabin's amalgam of music, spectacle and intuition at the dawn of the previous century antedates the multimedia actuality of the modern era.

Rear cover
Upper left scheme shows an approximate reconstruction of colour hues and the corresponding notes with their sound frequencies, based on Scriabin's indications. Lower left drawing, plate 39 (acoustic system) from Frank Netter [1977], depicting the point-to-point correspondence in high and low tones between the cochlea and the acoustic area at Heschl's gyrus on the supratemporal plane of the human cerebral cortex. Lower right, the colour keyboard, executed by the physicist Alexander Moser on Scriabin's commission and designed and constructed specially for the performance of the symphonic poem *Prometheus*, the first score to include a colour instrument. It is a wooden circle of twelve lamps: seven lamps according to the scale of the spectrum (red, orange, yellow, green, sky-blue, blue, violet) and five additional lamps linking the extreme colours of the spectrum and forming a transition from violet to red, rosy, rosy-red, etc. This circle corresponds to the circle of fifths in music, the red standing for C, the orange for G, the yellow for D, and so on [Hope, 1970]. The instrument has been housed in the Scriabin Memorial Museum in Moscow.

Printed in Poland
by Amazon Fulfillment
Poland Sp. z o.o., Wrocław